RISING THE PHOENIX

PATRICIA KATONA

Rising the Phoenix
All Rights Reserved.
Copyright © 2022 Patricia Katona
v2.0

The opinions expressed in this manuscript are solely the opinions of the author and do not represent the opinions or thoughts of the publisher. The author has represented and warranted full ownership and/or legal right to publish all the materials in this book.

This book may not be reproduced, transmitted, or stored in whole or in part by any means, including graphic, electronic, or mechanical without the express written consent of the publisher except in the case of brief quotations embodied in critical articles and reviews.

Vital Signs Press

ISBN: 978-0-578-27193-4

Cover Photo © 2022 Patricia Katona. All rights reserved - used with permission.

PRINTED IN THE UNITED STATES OF AMERICA

Rising the Phoenix
(September 2007)

A breath was drawn
   chest inflated
Defenses had been seized long ago
A lonely warrior stood atop a fortress
   With a pulse to echo through the senses
Eyes were clear now, the fog had drifted in
    Hovering among the lines
Cracked skin brought longing for moisture
   That pulse - it beat as thoughts forlorned
ALL
had been contemplated
A move must be made
   Weary bones, lengthy strides
 -Grabbed the hand
Little fingers traced 'round by promise
A seascape within the eyes

"Come along, for there is something I must show"

  'Tis my heart, a pulse
    Those eyes responded
Yet, there are wings
Softly, like notes of laughter on dew
The wings, their ominence unfolded
It must be so
   None receives such a gift and does not let it go
Rocking in embrace, we strengthened our plee
  Not standing as low, from this sight
Rid of a man
   He was never to Be.

Journey

There are certainly times when we find ourselves with the options of having either the perspective of: "Everything is perfect, I'm doing what I'm supposed to be doing and things will work out", OR the alternative of: "Screw this! It's not broke; I'm not fixing it!". Either direction offers a form of relief to the carrier of those thoughts and typically, the optimist in me decides on the former with sufficient reason and that gets me through.

However, as much as one might live in their mind and believe that the life surrounding them is sufficient testimony to their wants, when the reality of that life sets in and we're really nothing more than ANGRY — something has to change.

This is the beginning of what journey I've taken and how haphazard actions have lent themselves to a greater understanding of what it means to have to deal with the situation that you're presented with when the facilities that have been put in place to protect you have failed. It is a subculture that lacks empathy toward situations that multiply themselves over and over within a given society. It is also not accepted that the harborer and the protector of my situation (me) may be a slightly smarter version of your run-of-the-mill court attendee and therefore, poses a threat to that court.

Welcome to the journey as I attempt to make sense of the senseless.

December 26th

I was raped

Technically, I was still married.

Technically, I said "No".

Over, and over, and over.

And then I walked.

Into the roadway

Over my shoulder, I watched a light

My sleeping little boy would be okay.

I

Was not okay.

No preponderance of evidence

No crime.

Gray Matter

It is the struggle. The personal, internal struggle that keeps my mind buying back into what I already know.

It's wanting to know what he thinks, and answers as to why what happened, happened. What I really seek is an apology. He always fought dirty though, it didn't matter when we were pledged to each other - rather, me to him, him to whomever he wanted, when he wanted - why then would it matter when we split? Every component of life and self-assured strides that I held near and dear was viciously, publicly and cruelly attached to language that would deal out the ramifications for my life.

My ability to be a mother, to provide for my child, myself, my aptitude at work, choice of career, place of residence, my family and mostly, the way he would speak to me...over me, through me, as if I had no significance in his life; I had made no impact at all less being a bother, a bad decision. When I stopped responding (outwardly) he changed his tactics focusing instead on scape-goating our son in order that I might fall. Manipulation didn't work and so, deceit came in daily doses, cruelty established roots and honesty was absolutely out of the question. That still wasn't enough so upping his game, he moved to violence. I restate: more violence, and threats. Direct and indirect, they were both present. Harassment showed up hand-in-hand with abuse: 100-proof.

Brought up with a strong sense of pride and responsibility, I asked for help though I may have asked with too much independence - too much accountability, because it seems as though the powers that be, well they just sent me home.

Home to what? What home?!

I wanted, really, truly want(ed) to go home. Home to my family - home to some place safe where I wouldn't be stalked, threatened, thrown around or mistreated. I pleaded for my son's safety, took pictures every time another hand print showed up on his face, or arm, or backside. They always showed up. I listened intently to each horrible story about fighting, bleeding and words that cut deeper than bruises that had just started to heal. Between tissues and my blanketing sweaters, I dried every tear that fell, matching each with my own and rose to my feet to answer an interrupting phone call only to find that his father had joined his cause and now slung the same cruel, name-calling, heart-breaking statements in my direction.

Still, I tried. When he learned the word martyr, claiming he was not eating, not sleeping, that he had no food, I split my food into portions and filled a paper sack. "I'll be right up," I said. "I'll leave it on your porch".

He met me at the door that night, gave a sniff in the air and with the phone already in his hand, dialed the police.

Frozen in shock, I watched him eagerly express how scared he was for his safety / the safety of his child in my car since I had just showed up drunk and how I must be driving while intoxicated.

I left.

He got to keep the food.

And now...what is it? Five, almost six years later...I remember that feeling distinctly. THAT is what I couldn't for the life of me, figure out how to let go of. Today I had a little victory. Yesterday - I had one too. And tomorrow is promising in a wondrous way. My letting go comes from the way I define "holding on" and my victory resonates from understanding that I'm not in charge of much outside my walking, talking latitude to spiritualism. And from that I can say with all honesty that I tried every. single. time.

That I try still.

And each day is a promise to compassion and the unfolding of the blessed road before me.

Sunday, May 3, 2009

Affinity Apprehension

Suspect that there is a place unreachable by the hand, yet a viable option for release of pent-up aggression, agitation and elation. To what degree does this place allow for companionship of the physical realm? It isn't really somewhere that one would go to with any real mode of transportation other than the ability of cognition. Even so, it's threatening. It's a start; a beginning to what could possibly become a very hard fall for the other half of a story that's begging to be unfolded.

This place is a world of wonder, excitement and offerings.

Allowing anyone to be anything, it is solely dependent on the skills of its author.

My Exercise in Futility
(Originally published August 27, 2008)

My Exercise in Futility

I'm realizing that it's okay to be a little broken as I find myself very worried about the state of such a young one's mind - and may be more so, of the condition of his heart. Last night he uttered the words "hate" in a description of one who should be considered a young boy's "hero"...trying to make sense of it all, just as I am. Some tell me to see it in another light, that some kids don't have anyone to talk to. He has me, and oodles of people that love him and care for him - that with enough love, it will transform and that "every hurt becomes a muscle".

Still, the dust is kicked up whenever I hear another tale that somehow eluded me for these past few years - supposing it was my then naivete. The more time that passes, the less I even care to try and make sense of it. The less I identify - even that word, Identity - it is encompassing of he, the catalyst for Patricia. It seems, in my moments of confusion, that I'm torn between what my role may have been as "wife" and what I neglected to realize for my role as Independent.

I never saw myself, prior to materializing a "separation", as anything but a part of a marriage. This is necessary by definition and the need for two parts to complete a marriage, though if attempting to institute the morals of what makes a marriage (with two equal parts) then all efforts are futile. And to think that's what I was offered as insight on the day that I wed - "In order for this to work, each of you must be willing to give 100% of yourselves to each other".

Confident that I gave my 100%, I effortlessly loved. It was no more difficult than that, as I seemed to have been injected with a "love conquers all" inoculation at my early immunizations. What he failed to say was that if only one side gives their 100%, with no emotional income from the opposing side, then "ye shall be rendered as void".

All things become clear in time.

Return now to the mental state of a child with but 5 years of experience in this cyclical torment and you might understand my aggravation. That muscle growing from a field of pain, in concept, may have been applied prematurely. The heart's a muscle.

Enter irony and find that indeed by tending to my heartache and his five-year-old heartache, we are in fact preparing for a bounty of love to be timely harvested before the growing season is over.

Marked Mastercard

4 Years of Litigation: $20,000
Awards; Uncollected: $21,589
Number of Friends lost in the divorce process: 14
Having a Judge make a decision that's appropriate: Priceless.

Reading Backwards

Trying to decide what the best way to offer a proper introduction to my chaos is. There are more than three years put toward the effort of trying to have a Justice System produce something cumulative, accountable and right.

No dice.

I would offer that there are more stories than I could spend the time to write out in an evening and so, due to this craziness...I think that the best way to approach it is to offer the story from back to front.

Have you ever picked up a good book that you've heard was outstanding and though you were eager to read it front to back, your curiosity gets the best of you and you have to peak? That's what this is going to entail. We'll go slowly - and you'll be able to understand it from a perspective taken a step back.

Yea, that's what it will be.

Justice: Invert Style.

The Phone Rings
(June 2008)

...it's 9am on a Saturday, and I'm in desperate need of sleep, but I miss my boy - and so I pull myself to the receiver. It's him! He's quiet, submissive and (in my Motherly opinion) in duress. It's only a matter of minutes for our conversation to come to a halt by the atmosphere he must be in. I ask him what's for breakfast and the reply has to be reiterated to me in German - why? Because every facet of life there is controlled. It's like a substance that was never approved by the FDA - The Atmosphere.

Soon enough, it's too much to handle and G says his "good byes" - at which time the phone is handed off to the most-offensive of all conversationalists. "What's going... the conversation (if you can call it that, I prefer to reference such meetings of the mind as a kind of Pavlovian conquering mission.

I don't reply because I have nothing to reply with - and he really wouldn't want my answer anyway. Needless to say, there is no conversation with the Pavlovian Prodigy himself - it's a direct order in the form of conditioning and I'm not falling for it. Eight years of this banter; you'd think he'd redirect his attention elsewhere, but no - I must be his favoritest contestant. Anyway, it's thirty minutes of him telling me that "due to what G's been reporting is happening when G's at his house" that it has occurred to him that the problem must be because it's been such a long time since I've seen him and his child interact and that I must not remember the way he used to act around G as a baby.

Also, that there must be a tumultuous situation of abuse that has occurred to skew my reality and that I should seek therapy for the many plaguing issues that I obviously have so as to not confuse our son any longer - "It's that you're just like your father, don't you see that? You're incapable of accepting the reality of it all and you're making this stuff up..."

The suggestion was to "allow" me to come to his house to "observe" he and G's interaction so that I might "reaffirm my thought pattern " and re-examine my perspectives.

If I would be so kind as to do these things, then he would further assist me in correcting my ways and I would no longer be confused and make up the scenarios that have, for so long, been plaguing the lives of me and my son. It was quite obvious to him that it was only he that could take care of my woes and distinguish my thoughts to clear him of any injustice - but would have to be at the mercy of a PSYCHOPATH!

That's intelligent - let's just throw caution to the wind, shall we? Assume for a moment that years of physical, verbal, emotional and psychological abuse didn't happen and that I must have it all wrong. Assume that he wouldn't off me in a heartbeat if he had a chance and that he wouldn't take it out on G (afterall, he's only done it too many times in the past to keep track of) - and assume that he's telling the truth and that in my allotted hour of "observational" time at his house (where I was told that I'd have to show up alone and the "observe only" was specified) - that I could then rest in peace (If I'm not assuming that I'm already dead at this point) knowing that he's just as fucked up as I'd ASSUMED from the start.

What would that amount to in the book of accomplishments? (Assuming again, that I'm not already a goner)....Answers anyone?

To quote Ayn Rand: "Evil is impotent and has no power but that which we let it extort from us".

So, my answer (given the scenario of G being held captive in the atrocitus household for the weekend) was "No". And even then - No doesn't mean "No" to an abuser - it means that you're mentally weak. Too mentally incapacitated to speak further and say what you actually mean - which to an abusive psychopath means, "Yes".

I expect that he's awaiting my phone call or arrival.

This truly is an extortion of the soul.

Emotional Affiliations

I step outside with a wet head, draw my coffee to my lips, and realize that these are the mornings that I love. It is through the mist of the clouds, setting low in the yard, that the smell of wet leaves and dewy gloss waft over the grasses starting to turn to brown. There is the sound of birds rustling high in the trees and I take in a deep breath in an attempt to relieve this pressure on my heart. Many times, I can turn back the pages of my mind and recall the days that I would nestle into the crevice on your arm and wrap legs around in a mass of tangled morning warmth. I rest fondly with that memory and then suddenly, feel the pangs of love gone wrong.

It brings me out of that idealistic fairy tale and the clashing, banging horrors of what life was really like hits me square in the temple. That's the part that carries with it resounding pain. The kind of pain that I can't seem to drop now that I've moved on; now that I've been separated for more than three years; now that I haven't twisted legs with the man in nearly as much time as we were married. One would assume that things could be suppressed enough to dissipate after enough time has passed, but they don't. I'm finding that you have to pick them apart and dissect their innards in order to find the meaning to all the questions that surface when hindsight kicks in.

I talk to friends in a dire need to rid my soul of these horrors—wanting for the nostalgia of the good times to rely on and the bad days, the ones that dragged me to the bottom of despair, to go and eat themselves through until they don't exist. People listen—my friends, they listen—but I question whether or not they really hear me. The agencies, they're all set with convenient slogans of promise to help us through these agonies. They give tomorrow a shimmer of hope, but through my experiences, they lack a main ingredient. The one ingredient that extends achievement to make it real: accountability.

You retell your life so many times over to stranger after stranger with an undying hope that they'll be able to direct your sobbing soul somewhere profitable and yet, they jot down a few notes and schedule another appointment for some future meeting. My resiliency and idealism tells me that things aren't as they seem; that people really do care and that they are in their positions precisely for the reason to assist and amend. Why then, do they seem to take so long to realize that I am telling the truth? Why do I continue to feel the way that I do when I step outside and that dewy fog hits my face, the little pods of moisture stagnating on my skin and relentlessly wrapping me? Why is it that when I reach a point of clarity, I cannot maintain that perspective?

Maybe it is because memories play tricks on these dear hearts of ours. They plot and scheme and pose as benign stagehands for this play. I realize that in essence I'm living as though my life has already reached a pinnacle ending—its resolve to capture pain and heartache, wrapped eloquently in the warmth of a true love and a real partnership, has taken up residence in my void. In this cycle, I'm reminded that it is ultimately our choice to continue down the path of righteousness and truth; our choice to turn the corners of our mouths upward against that prick of painful memories—to prove outwardly that we will be alright in the end. I must keep in mind that those in the positions of assistance are there in order to help but they, too, are limited in their approaches. Friendly affiliations do not necessarily allow for a hug when we walk through the door of a practicing professional.

In this pain and heartache of remembrances, I feel I might reach a place where my strength out of pain will resound in my ability to stand tall on my own. In the meantime, I pray for continued strength and understanding. I reach out to the friends that smile cautiously as they listen to my tales of woe and I appreciate their place in my life. To build upon our lives is the essential part of living—the accountability that may be missing is what can ultimately be replaced and/or created by the ones that have trod this very road. In the lack of accountability on others' part, I take ownership of my life. I am building this piece by broken piece and when I finish, I will have created my own masterpiece.

"You can Have a Seat, unless you wanna be near the Ex"

Occurrence: April 16, 2009

Sometimes, when I'm feeling most drained and have to somehow derive power and initiative out of this ignorant context, I think about the players that are part of this game. This is their livelihood, what they do to make money and it's never-ending. As much as I disdain this process, it's not the entirety of my life. There's more than this back-and-forth motion that will grow into something substantial, beautiful, fruitful. It will not be like this forever - at least not for me, as this is just the fallout from a bad decision. This is the part where you're reading your script, preparing your costume and brushing up on your pronunciation when you know the last performance is coming up shortly. You've already decided that you'll no longer take part in this refuge of life, you're tearing up your advertisements and not circulating your name anymore for hire in this virtual exploitation factory. One more performance and then it's on to the "California" of your stardom dreams. One more go-around explaining the things that are so clear to you, but still remain foggy to everyone else. And it's because without having you as their actress, they have no cast to continue the play. They have no evil threads to weave; pitting ex against lover, against child, against mother. They simply have a script. Yes, you may be considered a pawn in this juicy game of mistrust, or you may be improperly cast as the villain when what you auditioned for was the opposite. They've already filled that role, and no one wants to be the bad guy. So, you play along knowing that you will unveil the real story in a fantastic twist near the unveiling of the plot. The type-cast persons will march out to the giant with mere pebbles and the rolling laughter from the hillside will suddenly be stifled when the monster falls. And won't it be brilliant! The audience, these puppets - will rise to their feet, clapping and crying, wiping away tears because Good did win out in the end. The lights will fade out, the curtain will fall and the dust of the production will be brushed from the stage. You're done. That was it. Time to move on to the venture of your "California" dreams. Time to rest, relax, recover and appreciate that you could see through the deception of the players, and of the play. Now - Now that we've got the emotional context out of the way - moving on to the anger of the situation. That's mostly the "dammits!" and the "What the heck?" - using more profanity than there are descriptive words ...say "court-system" and it's like my conditioning word to turn complete placidity into rage! We're working up to the descriptions on this one though - stay tuned....this poetic version of unfolding events shall soon take a new face. The one of itemized screw-ups of the litigation process, and of filing fees and attorneys/judges who've dropped the ball on more than one occasion and who probably couldn't spell my name correctly even now that I've spent the last four years with them.

I Love the Smell of Cognition in the Morning

You know that feeling that you get when you open your eyes just before the alarm goes off, it's silent and solemn, the lighting is perfect and your mind is at ease?

I don't have that.

Granted, I wake up before the alarm goes off. I even open my eyes to the greatest sight of the sun just coming up over the mountains and shining through my bedroom window enough to wake up the little critters that are scampering around. What I don't have in that scenario is the mental stagnation that I wish I could conjure up. Immediately, when my crusted peepers open, I have the reality shock-therapy treatment where my whole body reacts with, "Oh crap!" and the gears start turning. I'm remembering, reliving, reiterating and regurgitating at an alarming rate, and quite frankly…it's tiresome. I try to shut it off, make it stop – alter the course, and even start a new hobby to get my mind off the monotony, but it's still there.

I believe that much of what is, remains toxic at the core. It's like trying to find the one rotting potato in a bushel of potatoes. There's only one that's bad, but the smell is infusing the rest of them, and they all look guilty of rot. What do you do? Go through one by one and smell out the bad guy – what an analogy! Thus, the cycle of my time right now – it's really a RE-cycle. See? I'm "going green" and I didn't even know it.I don't mind so much on the good days – the days when I can wrap my head around it all; the effort that most others in this county are unwilling, or maybe incapable of doing. They don't want to wrap their heads around it. Why? Inability? Or just ignorance?

One in the same, I suppose.

Country Girl

There are fads that come and go and fly with the wind until they land on a group of people who all find the same line, same item, same idea exciting and invigorating until it outlives its welcome and then, is gone just as quickly as it appeared.

One such thing would be the titles that we give ourselves. They're used as an identifier. These titles are something that we can relate to, use as a conversation piece, find relative understanding with and allow us to be drawn to others who utilize the same descriptions for themselves.

There. Now we're all the same and we don't have to have any original thought.

I know... let's call ourselves: "Country, city, urbanites, Emo., Goth.", so forth and so on. It becomes a label of identity and gives us purpose. The problem is when we improperly label ourselves, our being – and that is not what we are amassed to be.

For instance, when relating to a certain teen that is nothing more than a student of modern-society and blindly follows the ideas force-fed to her from a wretch of a guardian – she deems herself to be a "country-girl". She is not. To suggest "county" is to present a concept that typically entails: honesty, trust, nobility, strength, honor and aptitude. Not that any other description would be anything less, and not that "country" doesn't also sometimes harbor other negative connotations, depending on whom you're speaking with. But to accept the term and more so, to use it to describe yourself, is like placing a piece of bait out there for other young and immatures to bite on – and it's not right. It's misleading.

She's sixteen, which in layman's terms equals = without ability to complete thought. The prospective bait is probably anywhere between fifteen years and twenty years old. Given the history of decision-making herein, it's not starting off as a promising venture, so I think it would be fair to say that there's cause for concern. Except that nobody really listens to that concern either. The whole world of online "bait and switch" runs like a deep-rooted malicious vein through the youth of our society, where they're learning the most improper ways to behave. What's acceptable, what's allowed and more-aptly, what's right, is replaced with "What's in, what's sick and what works".

Sadly, I wish for this young one that what will be hindsight (hopefully) will be foresight and that titles won't change what really is. To be proud of who you are, how you were raised and what your potential is to become, is normal – even encouraged. That gives us identity because it's a choice and it's afforded to us because we have free-thought. When we make proper choices, realize those that were mistakes and learn from each – that is growth. Aspiring to be more – be that "country" or otherwise, is a goal and thus, becomes an honest plan. But the blind, copy-cat actions are simply too dishonest for any personal progression.

Sometimes, it's worth Giving in

The matter of timing is what it was all about. That I'd fought so hard to find serenity when serenity was there all along — I'd simply misplaced it with the fortitude of my quest for justice. Justice doesn't always come with pushing so damn hard that you've numbed your feelings to the world. Often, it doesn't come with that at all.

Therein lies my lesson. The one that spit back at me and said "Stop!" I'd exhausted all resources that I didn't have at my disposal, and then I lay there, in disbelief. How had I come this far to be thrown back into the deep end? How?

I'm starting over with no expectations less those I place upon myself. Rather; self. To view through the eyes of someone unguarded and without prejudice. Especially the eyes of someone that doesn't judge "self" with such disrespect. That's where I think it will bloom. A small and subtle bud will begin to appear. I'm betting that by Summer, I'll be amazing!

Wednesday, January 13, 2010

The Unwrapping

I don't personally feel that the action of unwrapping gifts gets enough attention.

The act of receiving a present is something that we take for granted. We might shake it a bit, fondle it, tilt it side to side; listening for some obvious noise for a clue to the contents. The actual action of unwrapping the gift however, is lost to the greater desire to see what fills the question. "What is it?"

I propose that there exists an entire meaning of plausible retrospect in spending time contemplating each tear, rip or mauling of that gift. What is our best effort at undressing something new that we've just received?

On this proposal, I return to the substance of my unveiling in 2009. Certainly, it may be suggested that my attempt at unveiling is happenstance a little too late, but I'm recognizing that it occurred and that's where the power is. The recognition. Call it a shifty sabbatical, a minor excursion in mental-leave, or my vain attempt to take on the world all by my little self. Whatever it be named, I was absent for nearly three quarters of a year! I'm baaaack.

Let's see: January 2009 was beleaguered by an angry woman of scorned divorce who couldn't reconcile with the demons that she fought within = ME.

February brought a touch of ranting and tidbits of happy justification when I buried my head into quotes of strength and power. That didn't hold out through March however.

March 2009 - was somewhat tumultuous. My birthday month — and I couldn't seem to gather enough power to see that I was fast-approaching 30. That maybe I should be saddened by the prospect, or elated at the nearing of some right-of-passage. Whichever perspective, I just couldn't gather it. I didn't really care.

April came and brought with it a handful of friendly laughs and spirited attempts to be ever-optimistic.

I threw what is promising to be the first of a yearly "Effin Pity Party". This (I'm hoping) will become a weekend of tents and testifying to the martyrdom of self - maybe just for the weekend to let out what little pity we can gather for ourselves. Attendees shall be prepared to assist in offering pity to other members and expect such in kind. At current, the list of attendees is all but five - but we're funded by an entire society, so I think it'll get better with time.

And then, there's May, June, July...and through the Summer. Work. Work. Work. Good work though. I busied myself through the Summer months getting in touch with shoving all aspects of my building anger and contempt deep, deep down inside so that the outside world didn't have to contend with the issue that I was becoming. On the "upside," I found out that the depths of my irritability run far deeper than I would have ever guessed. Outwardly, I felt pleasant enough - showing just glimpses and peeks of what was hiding beneath. But inward — I was hardening like stone. The light - the pieces that held me together through the year were the unravelings of happiness and of family. The moments in Summer when the tire swing hung from the largest Oak tree in five counties, it rested at the end of its support. As if waiting to be played with...

In moments of losing it all, of losing my breath and finding it hard to breathe...I would look toward Heaven. And there, I would catch myself from falling. That sky; those clouds, they lifted. They floated free and unwavering from their purpose.

It is lifting.

Of all the times that I wished to float freely above my problems; my worry - I can attest to finally finding some peace in the unwrapping. I can say that I'm able to breathe without stuffing issues and without holding back.

The time unwraps itself. Sure, we assist when we push and beg and plead for answers. But we're coaxing in all the wrong directions. I scan through the pages of photos from a few mere months ago and realize that time is passing too quickly. That I've neglected to really breathe as an active, living soul. I've resisted a lung full of fresh life thinking that I was cognizant of being able to "stop and smell the roses" but my application failed miserably.

I'm stopping.

I'm letting go.

And I'm going to appreciate unwrapping the contents of the life I've been given.

Thursday, January 14, 2010

Me, Myself and I Meet Meta-Cognition

Language exists beyond the words that define it.

Language parallels contemplation and reflection.

It exists within the passage of time to be expressed through song, dance, interpretation, emotion and expressive ingenuity. If I would paint a picture of my very location, it would be that of a woman, standing atop a stack of three hat boxes. The uppermost one, slightly crumpled and faded. The bottom two are decadently adorned, holding each a head. Each head is filled with the contemplation of a thousand scenarios. Arms outstretched, she would be fitting her neck with the most delightful of the three heads and making another attempt to steep her thoughts in the tincture of some newly harvested lucidity.

There exists no bumbling of derangement, no clash of personalities, simply the fitting of cognition from one mind to the next in order to get an even-tempered flow of mental activity. The language would be ever-present, yet not involve any verbose. It may be a passive comprehension that what had just occurred had been a culmination of nearly three decades in the making. At which point, any on-lookers would nod in agreement, for they would have just witnessed a union. And like any union, congratulations would be in order. Me and myself would hold silent to their own stylish curve. They would graciously occupy the space that is hat box one and two; the foundation for the faded exterior, knowing that they would each gain a turn at being worn again. Right now however, it was "I" that filled the void.

Free-floating remnants of thought would hang in the air after it had escaped from the richly-colored and lavishly stocked hat boxes, carried on the wind until captured by "I" and toyed with.

"I" has created. "I" is being employed and "I" matters.

Friday, January 15, 2010

The Fallacy of Truth

Truth comes in several forms.

Truth may be absolute Truth, such as humans having a conscience, or the laws of science. Then, there is each person's personal truths; the truth that we believe as seen through the eyes of our experiences and our comprehension of those experiences. The essence of that personal truth may change, and actually, should change according to our growing cognition and how we're able to process our experiences as we grow.

In this respect, truth (as opposed to Truth) is fallible.

What we give power to today, as being steady and configured, may very well change by tomorrow.

In retrospect, how many times over the course of life thus far, have you felt as though your understanding of your environment was truthful and that you'd figured out how to put round peg into round hole, only to find out later that you were holding a square block...and that you'd made it fit?

This is where the component of change takes the stage. There is a point of reference which suggests that people don't change.

I believe that they do. At the least, that they are capable of changing.

I think that this element of change comes from the upgrade of personal truth. When we are able to reflect upon our basis for belief and reconsider its components, we are also able to modify it with new insight. Modifications, though seemingly small and insignificant can become monumental ingredients to change and most are derived intrinsically - in finding pleasure from ourselves. The opposing force being to placate our search with posers of pleasure.

In similarity, changes in personal truth may well render negative results, or digression. Reaching a point of depression, one might place no value in self, which would potentially extend outwardly from self into what that moment's truth is.

Within that truth is the tendency toward change.

That truth may come on suddenly, as with a tragedy or glimpse of death. These sudden and abrupt scenarios often give glimpses of inevitability; causing immediate change. Or the change may be a process of months or even years. When it occurs, it is as if waking with new eyes. Slowly and in masterful intervals, our change is threaded within every situation we've ever attended. Time in this place is but a concept to be set against our definition of time in our truth at that moment.

Essentially, isn't that our quest? To search for truth (and Truth)?

In that way, our quest, or journey is an ever-evolving and rotating set of definitions which we apply to the moments we live. Each moment is integral to the process of change; to the search for truth, even if that truth should (and probably will) change at some point down the road.

I pondered this as I walked. Stepping up another space, I awaited my turn at the register. In a robotic-like and contemplative way, I step forward, place my items on the counter, reach for my wallet and pull from it a crumpled ten-dollar bill. I hand it to the cashier. She places my items in a bag, gathers the handles and with an outstretched arm proclaims: "Here's your change ma'am"

And at that very time and space I thought: "Isn't that the truth..."

Wednesday, January 20, 2010

Eyes Open and Dreaming:
The Detriment of Insecurity

My confidence wanes today as my eyes flutter in the scope.

In a not-so-distant past, I can remember dancing in the morning; for the nighttime brought me great insight. It seemed almost second-nature to wake in the morning with a noggin' full of inspiration because of a dream. One that was recurring and full of elation. It was that of a little girl. Blonde hair, yellow dress and from ear to ear, a smile that could end a war. I would see her when I slept and I searched for her there in my slumber; always looking for anything to indicate her name.

Nothing.

In some instances, she was referred to as "sunshine," similar to that of my father. Green grasses and that flash of yellow that kept me returning to quest for the little girl of my dreams.

And then…it stopped.

I got no "goodbye", no "adieu" for now – nothing. I just didn't see her anymore. I'm assuming this is because of the emotional whirlwind that soon came to pass. Probably had something to do with the onslaught of four-plus years of trying to get divorced. Most-likely – that was the reason. And…as with depression and upset, often follows a boat-load of insecurities and the only action of placing dreams upon shelves. No dusting. No reflection. Just depression, without impression.

A recent reflection of mine as I endure to review my actions and how others' actions have impacted me, I find that sleep is calling for my return as well. That I might be able to catch my breath again. The confident, strong self took the reigns recently and aspired to forge through discourse. I let it. I've been coming awake and it's good. But today…today I'm feeling myself slip. My confidant self, I believe, may have gone for a bathroom break, or out to lunch. Regardless, I'm somewhat lost, and so I question…why is it that as soon as I begin feeling inspiration once again, and I check my feet; they're sturdy, as soon as I am about to exhale the deepest, fullest breath, it's as though I run over (and slam face-first into the ground) a trip-wire that no one told me about?! Unsuspecting fool.

Maybe it's a premonition (?) my dream – indicative of the freedom of a child, the innocence of being young. Maybe she's something to come. I hope she is. That was a large part of those shelved dreams…children. Of having children. May be more of the attempt to prove that I am a good mother. That I am able to give life to something besides my failed attempts at "fixing" everything else…the extension of family and of love…of what it means to be truly loved.

My vestige. That's what I strive to return to. Return to finding my dreams and I do feel it welling – that quest for "sunshine". Yet, I'm pausing because of what feels like inevitable doubt.

Insecurity. They battle…A LOT! Dreams and Insecurity, that is. For the record, I did happen upon an identifier for my sunshine: Thea –or- Chloe.

I like that. Makes sense to me. Makes me smile past my insecure frown. And I realize then, that there is much more of me that lies beneath the surface. I don't speak of it all just yet ~ partially because of the battle that ensues and part of it because I'm afraid to hear that my dreams might not be shared.

Sharing dreams ~ that's where the matter of life lies. And I so hope to share.

Saturday, January 30, 2010

Owned.

I have been lost to the idea of contemplation. The point in cognition where you're thinking about thinking - about every idea that's passed the realms of putting thoughts into their particular place. I've been categorizing and making sense of what I can, while hitting the "delete" button on the rest. Thing is, I realize that the mental trash bin hasn't been emptied. I thought that there might be some funky happenstance occurring that I hadn't yet accepted. That maybe there was a glitch in the wiring that wasn't allowing me to fully rid myself of these pesky little thoughts. They encompassed all those included in the "what if", "may possibly be" and "would have, could have, should have" categories...the "But..." situations.

At some instance in that realm, it occurred to me that it's all about what we choose to keep ownership of. What we accept as our own when it comes from the outside in. I think that we're highly sensitive-beings and more often than not, the influences of our environments bombard our beings with feelings and we process those feelings against what we think we already know. Against what portions of experience we have chosen to keep as our reference manual.

For instance: It has been said, thought and determined among the governing authorities that the placement of children on sleeping bags for an overnight stay with their grandparents, all in one room — is unacceptable. The punishment was governed by authorities who referenced some arbitrary set of something-or-others and the Nay-Sayers extended me a feeling that I'd done something wrong. And for whatever reason, I've chosen to live with that feeling for almost two years now. Until...I see the local news present (because of the single-digit weather that's hit our part of the state in the last week) that the homeless shelters are above their capacity. People are coming in droves to find a warm place to sleep and some food to eat. The camera-man pans over the crowd, who seem mildly delighted that they've been offered such a refuge and then I see it...a gymnasium floor covered with 2-inch thick mats for sleeping on; a wool blanket atop.

"That's it?!" I think. That government-funded, grant-accepting homeless shelter is providing beds and meals to persons (which, by the way, I completely agree with) and the "bed" as it would be, consists of little more than a mat on the floor?

"And I've chosen to keep lugging around this feeling of inadequacy because some person on a power-trip and in a so-called capacity to 'judge' has suggested that I acted unlawfully by having my children sleep in a sleeping bag, one room and during a visit to their grandparents'?"

Here I'd been searching for the next thought process that might offer liberation - and the issue of liberation has been to simply disregard and drop those "thoughts" as they occur. They are no longer owned by me as I'm choosing to disregard their existence and pertinence.

Okay to Feel

The power of letting go comes in the ability to feel without having to control where that "feeling" goes as you experience it. This came up recently in the event that called for attention from me on a level that existed outside the being in a room. When you're not letting go of all of it, you're crazy-making in your head and still trying to hold on to the control and of making reason where sometimes, there is none. Sometimes, it's taking that sigh of relief without having to explain beyond that. And that's okay.

In some events, in the process of letting go, it takes over the necessary element of really listening and of hearing what's happening outside ourselves and that might mean that we're not supposed to come up with a plan.

When you can't really listen and you can't really hear - when you're afraid of what you're thinking because of the chaos of what you feel... it's because you're digging your fingernails in as a last-ditch effort to attempt being the one in control. Be in recognition that you're not going to die for what you feel". And maybe that's part of the reason why the experience lacks explanation. Because it's outside of the self. Because in the process of decades of repressed emotion bubbling to the surface, there is no capable way of explaining it away or justifying it to the inquiring self that will equal enough of a reason beyond simply feeling it.

When that occurs — the point is to simply let it BE.

Indifference

Back to the drawing board where it concerns applying the self. In some certain situations, I think you try to care and you apply every effort of caring in an attempt to garner yourself an understanding, but it simply isn't effective...enough. Why is that? Why is it that you can even exist in a place where all you do is absolve yourself of the responsibility of being within an experience, and yet you still push for resolution though it doesn't concern you? Is that the power of having an integral position in something? Of being IN a situation and not living apart from it?

I deem this indifference.

A dangerous, suspicious place of occupying one's mind, indifference.

It's nearly a beast of its own. To want to have care, take care, give care and yet...nothing. Can indifference be tamed? Be logical? Be fixed? Does it evolve to the next life form that is...say, a touch of misunderstanding, or displaced anger, fear, rage? More of a want to be indifferent, when everything else is suggesting that you do care, that you do want "difference" in order to change indifference. I see that there is hesitation when indifference comes to play for the weekend. Like that friend that you don't really care for in most instances, but that you spend time with anyway. Maybe for lack of knowing what else to do with yourself while they're there. Maybe because they always seem to show up at the most-inconvenient times and force you to contend with the issues that are them.

Oh, indifference...why is it that I speak of you when your very nature is that of not caring?

The Elements

There were changes that brewed slowly - they took nearly a year to come to the surface in true light, bubbling ever so slowly until they spilled over the top of the pot in a rolling boil. Similar to the way that those "watched pots never boil" the adage to be calculated into the scheme of things once it makes sense in hindsight.

Friendships, they are like candy bars. Made of similar ingredients: chocolate, peanut butter, cocoa, oil and mix of those other names that you can't really pronounce. Some have nuts, some have spice. Others come with coconut and chewy nougat...they're all delightful in their own way, but there's always a favorite. A good and trusted stand-by that satisfies hunger when those chewy mixtures fail to fill the urge. This is the spin that bubbled over the surface. One of those "I'm thinking of looking to enjoy a new kind of candy bar in order to broaden my horizons".

I welcomed the opportunity and even drew on the strengths that were in the mixture. I put aside the begrudging after-taste and aspired to recognize what elements were really worth filling in the rating sheet on. In all honesty, there were many categories to that rating sheet that I added when I got to what should have been the end. I filled in more because it was worth it to me at the time. To have more categorizations of what my little candy bar could be - there was so much more potential that existed outside the 1. Satisfies hunger A: yes / B: no...2. Decadent mixture A: yes / B: no...and so forth. There was substance to the friendship and I had reached a point where the basic rating of beneficial - or - detrimental wasn't substantial enough to throw out the wrapper. You know; might wanna buy it again. Until now. When the pot boiled over.

Having invested more than the potential called for, I felt that I'd given friendship more than its due course to prove sustenance. I feel that I even mellowed out the taste with a bit of sherbet in between bites just to cleanse my palate so I wouldn't be judging unfairly. Then, there... at the crucial point of proving its worth, it crumbled. It blamed and pointed, accused and acted out. Dammit. Why?! I stated my peace. I've said my fair share where it concerns what the power of cocoa beans hold - and the ways that they can be so distinctly different, but still yummy. I gave chance, and chance, and chance...for the cocoa bean to come to fruition in its own time. I even waited. Damn cocoa bean. It's like waiting for a productive harvest from the orange groves of Florida this year; ain't happening.

Shame really, I was looking forward to having a new favorite. Guess that's why there's always a stand-by candy bar. Because some things never change - and others, the ones that do change...they're like a nuance to self-improvement. RE-focus attention where attention be: to the improvement (and change) only accountable to the self.

I didn't judge you little candy bar.

The 90/10 Principle in 2010

In many ways I am a creature fueled by fear, anxiety and low self-esteem. I gauge my own personal growth upon the "feel-good" measures that I have culminated for the day - only to find that there are far more triggers in my reactionary phase which I didn't give honorary credit to.

The 90/10 Principle basically states that life is made up of 10% of what happens to you and 90% - your reaction to that 10%. In measurement of reaction to circumstances beyond my control, I have failed. I have aligned my fear with the tally sheets that adorn my notebook for what I think should happen; consistently keeping track of the efforts toward self-improvement, and I recently slung a good line of BS at the person who is my hero because of it. The man who has, for four years been my daily breath of sanity, thick and thin, hot and cold, good and bad, he is there for me. Though as any wandering soul can relate, being bombarded with a constant barrage of "did me wrongs" gets old well before it becomes compelling.

Consequently, does one know what one does when one is called out on one's shit? I will tell you...

One that is fear-driven, denies the magnitude of one's shit.

After 4-1/2 hours of discerning this enlightened view point, I feel it fair to say that I have been a slow-learner in the category of what constitutes acceptance of mistakes.

I made a mistake. I played a tugging battle between the highs and lows which has kept this man chasing boomerangs for far too long! And at this point, the cryptic messages that actions were sending (even though cryptic) ...have served to adorn, or really cloud the intention.

Buggers!! In the meantime, and with 90/10 in-tote, I'm putting out there that my Hero deserves a medal. For contending with this, with me...thank you Love.

Making me Feel...

In a holding pattern again. Sometimes, it's necessary. To deliberate thoughts and feelings and properly place them where they need to go. In the context of time, I think that there's never enough to be completely satisfied with what you feel you've lost, but then again... too much when you're waiting for something else to happen. Frelling holding-pattern.

What we feel in many ways is a reflection of what and how we interpret another's actions and allow it to then impact our own status. Precisely what I'm having difficulty with. Yesterday, I imploded to the degree that there was nary a dry eye in the room...they sat, single-rowed and content until I opened my mouth. And it wasn't even planned — that "coming out" of feeling. The time limitations didn't seem to matter because there was a rapid boil of issues all competing for attention, or at least to be verbalized. So I spewed. Like a geyser...and it did feel good. To let it go - part of the reason that when you impart too much thought into any subject, your thoughts become the feelings that, when they're weighed against what you're intently trying to relay, are skewed. Gibberish that I can't seem to formalize into something constructive, but which I know IS constructive and needs to be lived through, contemplated and then brushed into the wind. For once and for good.

Standing For

Much of life is the capacity to stand for something, in favor (as it resonates with your personal philosophies) of an outcome that will most likely result in a general direction of "for" - OR - the standing against an opposing belief. In standing for, we create a constructive intent — the desire to see fruition as it would mirror our value

placed on the situation. And sadly, there's a realization that much action is invested in standing against things rather than for them. It's everywhere! Politics and media relations come to mind as the black hole of irritation. But that aside...

There's a sense of freedom when you align your cause with standing for the elements of power in your environment that they might produce something effective and beautiful. For instance, I stand for: the cause of open, loving, caring relationships — in love and friendship, I stand for teaching children that they have the power to view life in the most positive of scopes..through standing for.

It takes less energy to stand for and in the feng-shui sense, accepting the for from others is nearly effortless and creates a wholeness to the being. Standing against presents two resistive forces - kind of like running your car head-on into a brick wall. There's nothing positive that can be drawn out of that instance.

In the same context, introducing a situation that presents no resistance can often lend itself to be a scary endeavor for the immediate environment. Usually, and with the notion of "bird's of a feather..." having no resistance is a tool that comes across as being volatile... if that makes any sense. Either way, when you start the cycle, you perpetuate goodness. No more standing (against) the spin-cycles that serve only to drag you down. Circling the drain isn't fun for anyone, but there are some people that feel compelled to stay there — in among the hair and soap scum, pleading their case for being saved. If instead, they mustered up some strength of spirit, laced up their boots and went traipsing out of the scum...they'd be much better off. And in the event that you become aware of what it is that you stand for, only to see those around you standing against something else...well, march on little soldiers! Remember, there is no appreciation to be had for the self when you can't get out of your own way.

Contending with the Difficulty of Making Amends

Between me and my problem - we were entangled and confused.

Just because you want answers and validation and feel that by feeding me a continuous stream of unaccountability and confusion, does not mean that I must justify you with a response.

I would only be positioning myself and family for further ridicule as you would surely dissect my language and initiate your position of common pandemonium. Sadly, this is the interplay among persons with a waning proficiency at being honest, humble, or realistic.

As such, I have concluded that I shall not be burdened with expending energy in a black hole of rationalization.

Does then, our avoidance of showing affection to drama, mean that it will rise again in some new stage or forum? Probably. Only long enough to pull some of the air out of what exists as healthy — like fire starving for oxygen. It sits idle behind closed doors, under latched corridors and soldered openings until...until one day a window is mistakenly, forgetfully opened and *BAM* It ignites again!

Nope. Can't have that. Let the fire die out and don't feed it. Let it go until it breathes no life, affects no business of the current and decomposes to ash.

I suppose it comes down to the position of our focus. Focusing on the possibilities of fallout from any situation, instead of from the vantage point of the self (not in a self-conceited way), only leads to more confusion.

Lil' Piece of Heaven

I've got myself a little piece of heaven in my hand.

Those fleece sheets really keep out the cold, and as I unwrapped myself – planted firmly alongside my love, I gazed toward the window, the sun shining brightly in and calling for me to wake, I drew in a deep breath of life. Today was going to be delightful in all its mystery and story-telling. I could feel it!

I donned my best suede skirt, black, silk cowl-neck blouse, a pair of glittery stockings holding in the exuberance that my legs were feeling and slipped into my engineer boots just before putting on my green jade ring for the sake of its inability to absorb negative energy. I tossed back my blond locks (which are growing so fiercely as of late that I've decided even they're happy!), spritzed on my rose perfume and smacked my lips together with their shiny gloss just before looking one last time in to the mirror – "I love you" was the whisper and out I went to find my lovely, adoring fan base.

They were there – each of them in their wonderful beings. My Lovey – he's the embodiment of what it means to really feel love – to live love, and have it live back; love back. Take my breath away, that quirky, yet distinguishable, wonderful man! And he makes me laugh – like, really laugh, that guttural, belly laugh that sometimes stops all sound from exiting your body yet your mouth is gaping open. Ah, Lovey.

And "Wissa" – the pet-name received by little brothers that can't pronounce the syllables all the way for lack of their two front teeth. She's a doll – a beacon of what it means to be a young woman coming in to her own. So full of life – of questions and disbelief at times, and then others…she's whirling around in her pretties all dolled up for the world to see and appreciate. She's certainly appreciated.

Then there's "Dogger" – another pet-name not really befitting his uniqueness and brilliancy as a child - one with too many responsibilities and worries for being only six years old. He contends well for the most part though. If Lovey and I can keep up the positivity in our little home, it's sure to manifest greatness for this little boy. These two little cocooning larvae...we can only imagine what they'll metamorphose into. It promises to be quite a show however. I've already placed my reservations for VIP seating on this one!

Anyway, there they were – hustling, bustling into the beginning of this day. My rose parfum trailed behind me as I put together my coffee fix for the morning and stepped out the door to greet the day.

"Oh day of mine – how I've missed you!"

That's the summation – that this day is mine. It doesn't ask to be anything other than received. Another opportunity to jest into whatever we've decided is most important to our becoming; the day is there to grant that opportunity. And I'm joking. My smirky-grin isn't for the sunshine in my eyes, but rather in delighting for the opportunity to do this again. And maybe – just maybe, tomorrow I'll get to do it again!

From my Being

I've been here before. This very spot in my being where I didn't think that I had the gusto to continue. It was five years ago. And at that time, I didn't have the gusto. I didn't have care or concern, or even energy. It wasn't worth my investment to continue a relationship that had outgrown itself on one half and on the other, had dried like a shrunken head in the hot sun of life.

So strange to go around the bend after five years of treading water to find that the bend reveals a position of the being that I've seen and lived previously. At that moment, I do believe I felt my heart stop beating and because it had been beating in such rapid succession with the space that you occupy when you live with chaos, I had to make a decision right then and there. Was I going to live this cycle again, surely to repeat it over and over until I was no more? Or would I change up the game enough to realize my true potential at being? I let out a breath I'd been holding for years....FFFFFffffffff......

Change up!

Really, it was a dual-effect – a promulgation of forces all meeting at one location and smacking me about the head and neck to wake me up. I'm happy to say that it worked! I'd been sleeping; snoozing through the forks in the road that Frost's lines of encouragement delivered and decided to tread the same path; same cycle for years up to that point. Until I awoke, I didn't see that I had the man of my dreams, the life that I wished for – right under my nose! And then, the crusties came out of the corners of my eyes and I began to see – really see – what was happening. I'd become so accustomed to living in misery, that I called it company and let it stay for a while. Like that friend that says they need somewhere to crash, and that they'll only be a little bit…maybe a week or two. Until four months later, you realize the stink resonating from the couch is because they're still there and haven't laundered themselves. Aye! That was my misery – my company. Stupid, really. But at that point in life – it was elemental to sustaining anger and disbelief.

Around the bend I came – saw that same location, the same path – yet, this time…there was a fork. The fork symbolizes a necessary change – if I so chose to go that way – that I would absolutely need to push forward, no reverting back – no falling into the comfort zone of misery and chaos. Right now was the time to make it big and it HAD to begin with me. I would have to resign my position of being in charge and of redirecting every outside force to the cobble walkway that I was going. I would have to focus solely on M-E and not have it consume my thoughts of it being self-pretentious. Me had to be important to me and that couldn't happen until I began to give credit to the capabilities that I had in stock; untapped stock.

Two hands, ten fingers – gripping my chest for every fight left in my brittle bones, I grabbed hold and tore it open. If it was coming out – if I was going to be important to me, then I was going to get to the heart of the matter and really figure out what I had going on inside. I regurgitated everywhere! Imagine landmines of emotional disillusionment and sticky, yucky vengeance and baggage splattered on the walls and the ceiling, in my hair and on the light switch. I wasn't pretty. However…it was necessary.

The two months, three months that followed were assimilated to the processing of a seed that's planted in the ground in due time with the coming Spring frost. It can't germinate too quickly, or it'll surely die off …it has to get warm, feel secure, have the promise of Spring, get some water, some nourishment and then finally BUST out of it's little seed pod and with a click of the heels, find out just what it means to grow through dirt and become the rare orchid that it was meant to be! Badabing! I was coming alive and for the very first time in years; decades, I could breathe! No inhaling only to hold it – no exhaling frantically just to get it out …I had a pattern of breaths, deep ones and of generating my own sanity. Gradually, the corners of my mouth raised in a succinct pattern with the germinating thoughts of awesomeness that were in my head and now – well now I just can't turn it off.

I'm in love like Thumper in "Bambi" or the blushing little school girl that can't stop the twinkle in her eyes. And I'm proud. Proud of me – I'd thought for so long that my arms weren't longer precisely because they shouldn't be used to pat oneself on the back all the time. And now I wish that they worked kind of like noses or ears – and kept growing as we get older, just so I could give myself a pat on the back! Pat – Pat – Pat…there, there me.

I'm not done yet for this is just the beginning. I know this feeling, this life holds so much more for me, for us – me and Lovey – that it's going to continue to unfold in the most glorious of things. Sure, there'll be down times – and sadness, but in the correct mindset, it will be handled in the best of ways, healthy ways. I'm an active agent in my own life and I owe much of my gratitude and accomplishment to the man that (through threatening the very worst) peeled back the layers of my onion skin and held my feet to the flame; Lovey. For you – I am so graciously thankful from the depth of my being. You are my one, and hand in hand we'll travel this awesome, beautiful life!

Dear Self

It is precisely at this point in time that you need to be reminded of some very dear attributes and coincidences that affect your being.

You are no longer subject to the hassle and persecution of your other being – the one that has kept you prisoner for far too long to the scrutiny of your self. You have broken free from the chains that bind in that matter and you've been afforded another opportunity to live your life "as if". In this calling, you shall immediately begin every action as-if it were for the best of every dream and desire you've ever had. There is no judgment that will take from you another ounce of energy or life force, it is not allowed. There is nothing that can return you to the point of a critical state of breathing for you have weathered the storms to this point and you've been handed the "pass Go, collect $200" from your maker.

Your life as it was is not your life any longer. It has bearing only to the point that you remember the nuances which guided you; that you recall the elements that were so harsh that with the deepest breath of air you know you will never have to live that again. NEVER! You shall discontinue visiting that place that harbors pain and anger to the point that you are rendered helpless. You are not helpless. You are not a victim. You are strong and come in a complete survival package, full of the accoutrements that every "backpacking-through-life-being" needs; even the little matching blue-speckled cup and saucer set.

The path you've trod to this point was orchestrated in such a manner as to teach you all the core elements of moral and ethical masters. It was no mistake – and for the record, you passed. The intention was to get you to learn and to foster belief that you absolutely can make it through your storms, no matter what degree they reign down upon you. From this, you've garnered a new outlook and understanding – you are stronger than you ever gave yourself credit for and more beautiful when looking from the inside-out. You cannot gauge your actions through the eyes of others – only through yourself and from this you will find great peace and serenity at knowing you are exactly where you are supposed to be. You exist in the plain of a beacon – showing to others what it means to live a good life and though you get weary, your purpose in life is beyond measure. You have been looking for a quantity that will make it all "fair" but there is no fairness when your footsteps have precision in their step and intention in their making.

Keep walking as if – and everything – absolutely everything will unfold before your eyes. To such an extent that the words will elude you for description and your senses will be filled with the acknowledgement that purpose has found you and you are home.

Four, three, two...

I don't know exactly where it started: the fear. I believe it to have been something like that of a constant drip. It began and just didn't cease; drip, drip, drip, fear growing as I tried to balance curiosity with learning. It was a matter of waging war between heart and brain, of that I'm certain. Brain urged reality, desire for freedom and suggested ways out that would surely leave me as emotionally-void as he. And heart – well heart may have helped the drip of fear more than it was entitled to. It too, was scared. Mentally, I can picture it as the scales of justice – or as it would be at the time; justification. Everything from the sociopathic stance was justified to me: so much so that the directive soon came to: "Write down what I say. That will enable you to go back through and remind yourself of what your problems are".

That was nearly ten years ago. And those novels that were to serve as reminders – they've been burned to ashes.

The thoughts however, stir. Like dusty, clinging webs of pragmatic demise, they hang in the far regions of my mind. "What my problems are…?" What are my problems? I can see now what they may have been then, but do they still infiltrate my actions now? I think it's like the teachings of the power of the unconscious state: that we all bring a program of hopes and dreams, of fears and behaviors with us as we transcend into adulthood; into relationships. It's unconscious – it's seemingly subtle and yet, like a vapor it interrupts our adult lives with the search for unmet childhood needs, not recognizing boundaries or walls.

Drip, Drip, Drip.

The webs are relevant because now and again, I take a mental broom to them and open the windows. Their relevance serves to remind in a positive way – to remind that at that time, and maybe even now – I am too kind. I listen, (stubbornly) I engage (directionally) and I anticipate the outcome (prematurely). I expected promises to be fulfilled and carried out. I anticipated the day when all sorrows would be forgotten and when I walked to the mailbox there would be the grandest, most golden invitation to a celebration in my honor. TA-DA! An apology might soon follow for contending with all those things that hurt and traumatized, that injured and frightened me and being that I was so forgiving, I would take my golden invitation and check, check, and triple-check the date to make certain that I showed up early for the big day. That day didn't come though…and it never will. Not in that regard. Because it's been lived; that facet of my life – that experience and all the tools, tears, fears and happiness that it brought with it has been lived. It creates cobwebs at this point and some I keep, but most go through the open window.

I anticipated that there would be more sorrow than this. And maybe it's because I held on for far too long – wanting for things to change and be what I saw them as in my mind's eye. They couldn't possibly live up to that expectation, ideal as it seemed. And now…now it's a cartoon of sorts. The memories – the ones that must go now, they hang with four fingers clutched to the edge of a cliff. I'm above those fingers and one by one, I pluck them off. Four…three…two…*BINK*….they fall away.

A Way

There has to be a way out of this stalemate.

Is it just me who's feeling the beckoning of desire up against the drag of communication? Doesn't seem to be productive in any way – this attempted "fight no more forever" deal breaker between the ex and I. I'd be all for putting down arms, and basically have – but him: he seems to embody what it means to entrap, con, manipulate and belabor. Bah! Move along I say! Move along to a time in your life where you're actually living it out in the scope of what it means to be you; not me, not through our child.

More about me: about how I can alter perspective, how I am able to accept life and change it into a fine pair of spectacles for viewing it through. Of how I choose to accept language – language of love and life and of dispelling fear. Fear governing much of what happens – that we might not account for enough, harbor too much pain to be inoculated against it and at some point, after years of treading life's waters, that we might not have enough air to breathe until we get to shore. Silly fear. Such a waste.

You know what was exciting about Ginger being the barefoot temptress and askew chanteuse on an island? It was that she trod on her own desire in light of the circumstances of her train-wreck existence. For a character designed on sarcasm and a sharp tongue, my identity met its match and then it transcended to another level, as dear Ginger donned her gown and traipsed into the next melodramatic scene. I effortlessly apply too much thought into what it means for something to have meaning.

Open mouth and express a new found liberty of perspective and wishfully waiting to hear feedback, I sit.

The circle-'round effect is squared off at the shoulders of making peace with my demons. Most of whom have already vacated the premise, but still – a few remain. They may always be the stow-away kind to "poke" attention to things that should have died long ago; ideas, thoughts, memories, etc. Acknowledging them just enough to kick them out of the way. They've been worried over enough – given enough time and energy and no longer are they mine. They just happen to reside in the deep, dark voids of my brain.

A Chance at Redemption

It came to me today as I followed a little red-winged blackbird that's been flitting around the nearly-empty parking lot in the back of my building. It flew among the branches of the trees; the poplar's all shedding their fluffy seed pods left the bird scampering through what looked like snow falling mid-Spring. I'm searching, longingly questing every time I get to thinking – always thinking that there must be something I'm missing or an element of this picture that has escaped me.

Like the bird however, the one that skipped branch to branch – I'm reminded that much of what I'm aspiring to be, I already am. I fail at giving myself credit because I don't want to be boastful and then the second-guessing starts. And well, that's a never-ending cycle. I keep assuming that I'm going to end up at *that* spot where I'll be happy and the efforts that I've put in will render a beautiful result of life as I see it in my dreams. In essence however, it's already arrived – just that the thoughts I'm having are overwhelming (and ultimately creating) the vision that I'm seeing.

Manners & Comprehension

One thing that I fail to understand is how I spend inordinate amounts of time to consider what I feel are the various avenues of possibility and yet, my expectations are often rendered a dry well. What is it that I'm not seeing? Did I miss something? Am I still supposed to be hibernating? Can I please get an answer? Someone…anyone…

This cycle of communication mishap, the one between me and the "system" seems so hindered that I retreat. I draw back the reins and pull under my shell to contemplate the pieces that I may have overlooked…how I might be further persecuted and what that would mean to accomplishing a dear goal of mine. When I feel that air has cleared and the smoke has dissipated I venture out again.

BAM Miscommunication in my face!

Posh.

Bah.

Voltaire said that "True greatness consists in the use of a powerful understanding to enlighten oneself and others", and though I perfectly understand that, I feel that my comprehension is belabored by the others. And how is that right? What I understand is that there is a large populace that remains blissfully ignorant, that as much as I attempt to follow rhythm, my step is heavy and that language is key to communication and is highly gauged by the manners that are instilled in that language…or else tone.

Maybe we can start there – with communication. "Please" and "Thank you" are both incredibly powerful and when you couple the basics of language with priorities, well…then you're on to something good.

I figure it can't always be like this, not forever anyway. "This too shall pass" was a common phrase as I recall my teenage years, spoken often by my mother. And yet now I sit with the hope that "This too shall pass soon" - as my patience is wearing thin; my comprehension even thinner. Oh, and "please".

Dearest Child of Mine

I am sorry that you have to contend with these issues that exceed your cognition right now. I'm sorry that I married a man who has not produced a good role model for your fragile state of mind. I'm sorry to see you weighing the good against the bad and not knowing where to turn or what to do. I'm sorry that you feel like no one's listening. I'm sorry that there isn't change coming faster and most of all, I'm sorry for the times when I don't know what else to do or say. I'm sorry that he's broken.

I'm glad that you feel safe enough to act out around me because you know you'll not be hurt. I'm glad that you're blessed to be as intelligent as you are. I'm happy to see your face shining on the good days and humbled at your smile. I'm saddened to see so much hurt put in your direction by someone outside my control, but delighted to see you growing into a wonderful person who is more compassionate than you are resentful.

I pray more than I answer and try to be thankful more than I worry. I do have absolute faith that this will not last forever and that every dream is worth following. I recognize that this will not be the last time you have to come up against forces outside your control or understanding and that the head-on meetings with the man who fathered you, will certainly occur again. It is my job to prepare you to work through these inevitabilities in the best and healthiest ways possible for the tools you're equipped with and the age that you are.

It is what we fear that we are gauged emotionally. Or, in reference to the Piscean me…I've gauged everything emotionally, fear or not. Bugger. With that in mind, there is a path that unfolds before me, it's been a tad rocky and overgrown, but a path nonetheless. I'm referencing this path because it encompasses the dear message, the continuous worries and the frights of childhood that I allude to with nearly everything I speak of. Bah.

Tomorrow…maybe tomorrow we'll speak of confusion and what that means.

Be the Drip

Because parenting was never described as "easy" and because the added element of divorce, makes nearly any nuclear family with children become mismanaged, I am having a difficult time with being Mom.

I don't believe it's the adage of "Because I said so" 100%, nor do I think that children should be handed the reigns of their childhood to run amok as they choose. I don't know that there's any one ideal that I subscribe to with parenting, and I have yet to meet someone who has raised the perfect child. As a matter of fact, there appear to be more parents that are still searching for clues to living as an excellent human-being, than there are children (me being one of those).

I don't mind the every day cycle, the running, the gathering, the shopping and the structure; what I mind is the incessant evil and manipulating nature of "the other" parent that appears to act only out of spite and vindictiveness. Isn't there somewhere he can go? Like… the tar pits? Or Iceland?

It was about a year ago that I had an inordinate amount of tension pent-up and decided to take it out on a dried out log that had been sitting by the fire pit in the backyard. With a splitting maul and an ax, I marched right over to it, read it it's last rights and then commenced the pendulum swinging; hell-bent on finally splitting it to handy little pieces for the next get-together. As I'm sweating into my swing, I hear a *tink, tink, tink* from the side. And any wood-chopping person knows that you keep an eye and an ear out for what might be around you as you're lunging blade into wood, so as it would be, the noise was slightly disconcerting. At the turn of a head, I see my bestest girly – she's in her strapless sundress, hiking up one side with her left hand, barefooted and *tink, tink, tinking* at the other log nearby…with a bitty, little ax. The wood slivers flew into the breeze as she held her dress up and out of her way – you have to plan your trajectory, you know. I made a comment to her that day being as frustrated as I was … "We're all about futile efforts here!" We laugh about it still. The picture though – of taking measures to just keep chipping away at the problem, the goal or whatever other name you give it…I suppose that does have an effect; futile as it may seem.

Like Peg told me over a year ago – "Be the drip, Trish!" She used it as a metaphor for how the tiniest amount of water can create a cavernous ridge in solid stone just by dripping, continuously and without diverting from the drip…drip…drip. It's back to the making of life, as compared to the dredging of life. I'm tired of dredging. Time to kick things up a bit (or at least get my *Tink* on!).

Polish Up Those Shoulders

Today I was asked when I'd be taking "that trip down the aisle"? At this same time I was reminded of the ways in which we process relationships and how, for whatever the reason, things have taken their sweet time in coming to fruition. Relationship-wise, you're either the "point-and-shoot" type where very little nuance, every bothersome issue or habit is because of something that someone else did. Or, it's a role-responsibility relationship.

In many painful reminders I believe I've succumbed to the ever easy point-and-shoot and I would imagine that's because the alternative is hard. If you accept the responsibility of your role, rather than pointing a finger whenever you're displeased, it becomes fairly evident that it is you who must do the work.

Not afraid of work, I put my gloves on, preparing to identify the problem and drag it out by its toenails if it didn't voluntarily go. Ask Lovey - that poor man's been through what might suffice for a modern day war of the roses where it concerns my stubborn streak and cleaning-frenzy-when-agitated therapeutic regimen. And though even that can have its good side (streak-free living quarters) I begin to feel pressure when its all the time my problems, my issues, my therapy, my mental health, what I'm working on fixing, etc. I begin to feel as though I cornered the market on tumultuous relationships and anecdotal self-help.

Rationally speaking, I know I'm not the only person that has issues they need to work on, and I'm certainly not the last, yet depending on my focus, remembering that rationale can become very blurred. Resolved to stop pitying myself, I take a deep breath in and conjure up the energy to step forward again.

"Alright" I tell myself, "you're going to have to accept this one too. Polish up those shoulders...". There were times when the little things that played out in our lives as children implanted themselves so deeply that they became seeds for our adult actions. Only at this stage does one realize that by correcting the faults of those before us, we must also acknowledge taking the blame for it as well. And isn't there some adage about "with great responsibility comes great...?" I think Spider-man said it. "Power". So power it is.

Ultimately, I am responsible for how I feel and to what degree. I know that I feel happy when I have the love and attention of my partner. I know that I feel gracious when I have the health and togetherness of my family and children, or when my son sleeps in my bed because he's "not scared there," (even if it has become a last resort for convincing him of an early bedtime)...or when my photo albums reflect the years of memories in all stages of life. That entails a role-responsibility relationship; therapy being an added bonus for years to come. Being careful of the pressure that I exert on someone else making me happy, I'm going to have to keep my role(s) in mind.

And in this same pattern of thought, I'll dream forward to the day when I actually am walking down that aisle.

Boy; Unhinged

"…and suddenly I was exhausted by all the years I spent doggedly chasing the carrot of self-improvement, while dragging behind me a heavy cart of self-criticism" (Bremer, K., 2010, Excerpt from Cover Girl).

Ample enough to be a maverick rather than gauged by the illusions of society, to which one can never fully measure to, I've gathered a resounding quantity of stillness in this day. It wasn't more than a week ago that the pangs of doubt were sucking the life-force from me and but 12 hours since I last breathed that heavy-handed sign of desperation. Criticism and self-improvement are oddly paired in what trails through my day and somehow, self-improvement wins by a hair's breadth of distance generally leaving me to slump into a mass among twisted sheets and the ceiling fan whirring its meditative noise for me.

Rett was but one when we began this flight of fancy. Bitterness and rationalization soon came to the surface, followed soon by a mix of fright, pain and anguish. When I can project the timeline in my own head of what he's had to endure through what constitutes 90% of his life, the results are debilitating. I can only imagine what his adult therapy sessions are going to sound like should he ever muster the courage to delve back into his childhood once we finally get through it.

Where do you start something like that? "Once upon a time in a state of confusion and mistaken identity, I was born…" that's how I'd begin that phase of treatment.

See what comes of it from there. Posh.

It does lead me to thinking though…what exactly does self-improvement consist of? What do you temper it against? Yourself? Your self? (I always preferred to reference the self in that manner. Don't really think it's appropriate in a grammatical sense, but for the sake of the psychoanalysis behind it, I feel it's much better to separate the two – you know: my self, her self, your self, etc. The self as it would be, is a separate and highly important position.). Little perennial that he is, Rett has this amazing ability to switch modes from one to the other depending on his surroundings. It's becoming more and more prevalent - either he's happy, young, curious and free when he's home, or he's returned from a visitation in a state of fright, fear, angst, anger and self-protection. Now and again there's the marking that indicates Dad wasn't able to control himself (this "self" stays with the "him") but as my little perennial builds his vocabulary and personal identity, the actions of Daddy dearest are more and more psychologically twisted.

Really twisted.

Yesterday, for instance, was a good day for him. He was home. He was safe, unburdened with what he had to process and how much it wouldn't make sense to him. He was free to tie up his shoes and run through the fresh-cut grass with his dog. He sat for dinner and said grace without peeking out through interlaced fingers to make sure he was in good company while doing so (Saying a blessing is forbidden at Dad's). He was a boy, unhinged.

Today, and at the notice that he's scheduled to spend the long holiday weekend with Dad, like a light-switch he transformed. All that aggression, those questions, the worry…it's been building since I gave the news. My correspondence with his teacher through the day has already revealed two emails that speak to him "being unkind to a classmate" and so full of energy that he can't "sit still". He KNOWS!

"Give him credence!" I think to myself. "He's not just six, he's six and intelligent! He's confused and receiving empty promises. He's scared and not getting safety. He's voicing the injustices and not being heard!"

That. Is self-improvement. It's self-improvement being cut off at the knees, but self-improvement nonetheless. The catch will be if he can continue to improve himself and make the changes to not pull a wagon of guilt behind, or criticism, ... or anger. Already, he's farther ahead than most. Somewhere though, in the midst of learning your voice and learning yourself (while learning to live in your circumstances) I believe you are more-likely to be recognized by your age than you are your intelligence, particularly if you're "too young". Bah.

Hinging this child is the necessity he faces to swing between the highs of "normalcy" at home and the enfeebling lows that come from time spent with dad. From that I sit in a state of stillness today; figuring that when the time is right to move, I can be reassured that there is more faith than fear. Or as T.S. Eliot said, "Still and still moving"...there is movement though in the physical sense all is still. There is movement. Enough so that when this cycle finally spins out, my little Rett will once again run as a boy; unhinged.

The Web

I don't recall it having started this way. You know, me: being pummeled through the universe with a milkshake in one hand, pen and paper in the other and all the while, attempting to maintain my sanity. I believe the purpose was to experience growth as it would be similar to the flowery expressions you find on bus stop posters or billboards lining the highway of life. This though; this is for the birds.

In one aspect, I feel pressure on the seams of my garments – pressure from elatedness, being happy and having faith that everything's working out as it should. On the other side of those same garments, I feel the prickly sense of: anger, hurt, futility and an arm-load of that wrinkly face you get when you're biting your tongue and cursing under your breath. That part usually comes out in a sarcastic sense of wit and charm.

The time span of this chaotic sensibility began years ago and somewhere in there I recall having the thought that the huff and puff of getting things done always seemed to land squarely in my lap. I didn't mind so much at an earlier age because I could handle it, I welcomed it. I wanted to have the opportunity to prove I could do most anything. Now though, now I feel as though I've documented the pleadings of a sycophant and have to somehow remain on course while making efforts to get off the bus! I went to the doctor at one point – finally accepting that I was upset and depressed... that I'd cornered the market on not being able to sustain my innate sense of happy-go-lucky and somewhere deep inside, I was dying a slow, horrible, stinking, rotting death. I remember that day too: the day I walked in to the doctor's office and hung my head to save the receptionist from seeing the dark circles under my eyes, or that she might assume (correctly) that I'd been crying for a good, long month's worth of time. Either way, the doctor appeared – listened to my story, (P.S.: I initiated my consultation with a "I think I'm depressed") she made some medical hieroglyphs on my chart and then suggested that "I think you're depressed...have you tried a calming bath? Do you get enough sleep? Maybe you're not eating properly, etc.". It was more debilitating if anything. At one point in time, the doctor did recommend that I get on some heavy medication, but I could just imagine that one coming to surface in the realms of the court. Lovely.

I did contemplate eating the "calming bath salts" at one point just to overdo it on sodium, but I believe I ran out of energy there again. Then there was the idea that sprung to life – I had decided that just to get someone to listen, I would pack my trail-blazing backpack and camp out on the steps of the county legislature building until someone had me removed, or pulled up a cot. Either way, I figured, they'd have to listen. They didn't.

I conjured that I would begin painting billboards to place in my own yard – things that would read "Abusive Man Gets Away with Not

Paying Child Support for Years", and "How to Escape Accountability: Live Here!", a "Can't Keep Your Hands Off Your Kid? Get on the 'Fathers' Rights Train!", or "Do-it-Yourself Widowing Company. Inquire Within"…but decided against my better judgment on that one too. Really, the whole point was (and is) to get someone to listen…. someone, anyone, somewhere please just listen!

'Round about that time, I landed on one of my best analogies for the tumultuous state of affairs that is being married to a madman and the subsequent child-rearing and divorce that follows: The Web. The Web, is the idea that I'm walking through this fiasco and like would be when you've stepped into a spider-web hanging almost iridescently in the trees…where it spans across your face and you feel the snagging tentacles of it between your eyelashes and around your mouth…that you pull at it. You make grand gestures of swinging hands and fingers to try and remove it from your head, but you miss. You keep waving arms and hands, wanting that eerie feeling to be removed from your life, from your person. You can feel it, you're living it, and it's there right in front of you…but to everyone else - everyone that sits on the side lines or can view you from afar…or can hear you, see you, know you – all they see is you waving like a lunatic. And because the mass populous really doesn't enjoy spending much time investing in prosperous cognitive energy (i.e. to think) … you are nuts.

With that in mind, I'm investing in that awesome spray that they use in the movies. The stuff that hangs on the invisible rays of an infrared sensor so you can see where the lines are as you're pulling off a jewel heist. That's what I need…spray it on my face and *BAMMO*!

Proof.

That is what I've been saying, doing and relaying all along: THE TRUTH!

Invested Energy of Focus

The way that I see it with my "mind's eye" is that my brain is compartmentalized into many, colorful, and oddly-shaped boxes. Some have trinkets of memorabilia; some have Swarovski crystals, while others are ink drawings, covered in dried flowers and decoupaged to the hilt. They're all representative of some mode of thought-process and are often called upon when the subject matter fits. There is no "round peg; round hole" synapse here…it's strictly dependent on will, emotion, energy and incredible accuracy. The placement of each thought or engagement of activity has a reference point of subject matter in those colorful little boxes; similar to that of a cognitive card catalog. And the point of all of this is that when something occurs and needs to be referenced, responded to, reacted on or have mental reflection, I go to what I know. The problem exists therein. If you're made aware that what you know is dysfunctional - if you're reference table is devoid of purpose any longer and if you're effectively responded, reacted or reflected on something that has served no good purpose, how does one eliminate that strain from the brain?

At first glance, I would assume that you would simply stop referencing that same old way of behaving and reacting. But it's proven that our little computerized brains create synapses of connectivity for thought by the history that we've engaged it to; a self-conditioning, if you will. So, then the question becomes "how does one un-condition?" Maybe it's like a computer disk and formatting it to erase all the old data and would-be information. I've got to figure that one out – how to format my brain waves. Not return to the same course of thought, action or process that I've done in the past – the ones that simply do not work.

I suppose that as I contemplate a new way of approaching the old and of creating new, I am engaging the new as we speak. Don't wonder so much how to do it since you're already doing it.

There was Him and There was Her

He did ask.

In all fairness, he asked before too.

"What's the matter?" or "What's wrong?"

Her answer always seemed vague and obtuse and for this, he'd get irritated. It seemed as if she wasn't sharing, or that she didn't know. And really, that was it - she didn't know. No one word could embody the helplessness and judgment she experienced. Not only did it seep from her pores, the trepidation would drip from her fingertips or tear from the corners of her eyes with the slightest of cause.

He'd think that he'd neglected something, forgotten or entangled some problem - but it wasn't him. She loved him so much that it hurt. And there were days that came and spoke to her: the feeling of freedom in one person, of finally finding what had for so long been sought - her Love. Mentally though, the words to explain to him... they were caught. They were jumbled. And for all the worry; he knew this. He wanted with his every effort to make it all better for her.

But he couldn't.

Sitting in her garden she could tell that he tried. She watched him come to her in sweetness and just smile. He'd given up asking what was wrong since the last time her explanation came out sideways. Shame. For she certainly loved to hear the care in his voice when he'd speak to her. Shame that experience conditions the heart.

She pulled the weeds that choked out the brightest greenery in her garden and thought that one day soon, she would be able to hand him an invitation with all the right words. It would be perfect with gold lettering and flowing design. It would have space and comfortability - it would be welcoming, promising and undoubtedly ideal.

She would invite him to be her husband, to take her heart and protect it well.

She would promise the same for him.

For as much as she didn't know, the one thing that she could count on as sure as rain was that for her, he was perfection.

Be Not...

There is a bit of simple serenity when jaunting through the woods after a summer rain. Behind me, trails the dog; nose feverishly smelling for a trail that may lead to some grand find...and my son. He's seven and as such, has a capacity for language that I don't quite recall having at such an age. It may be that the synapses are firing much more quickly than his gum-filled mouth has time to speak, or that he's simply a spontaneous conversationalist. As it was, we trod in our flip-flops with but one, small hand trowel and the want to find a native plant that might suit our myriad of gardens in the manicured landscape of a backyard.

The hound happened to sniff out a plethora of deer droppings and skittered away whenever a branch would snap, or a leaf would rustle and my son only seemed to find every poison ivy plant that exists this side of the reservoir. Nevertheless, it was serene. Imagining a time when the worries of parenthood and adulthood might be behind me, I figured that there is cause to stop and take in the space around. As much as the days take up the time for working, the evenings following supper time are somewhat of a lost art form. Although it did work to our advantage that dinner came earlier tonight, rather than the usual 8pm time frame that we have to work with.

Lovey and I spoke of instituting the much-sought-after summer delight of "Sunday Sundaes" again. A wonderful idea brought on by none other than Grandma — Sunday sundaes are just that...a call to all family members to Grandma and Grandpas on Sunday afternoon, armed with a sundae topping of choice. Grandma supplies the ice cream and among eight siblings and significant others, we cover the gooey, chocolatey, nutty goodness (whipped cream too!). So, after the search for greenery I'm thinking that there must be the priority of making up for lack of Sunday sundaes and making the time for jaunting ~ flip flops, or not.

The Evolution of Fireworks

My thoughts remain somewhat obtuse this morning. They're circling a vast theme of characters, references and time frames in the process of marrying young and divorcing early – of beginning a family and dropping dreams – somewhere among the process of becoming I've concluded that this really needs to materialize into a book. The raw materials are mined and lying atop the minefield, wanting for harvest. I'm just not sure how to place them all into a congruent timeline of events.

I return to the whole "If I were to paint a picture of my mind's eye" explanation where that picture would be something of a woman jumping through the universe, attempting to collect the sparkly remnants of a firecracker; a big one! Drawn to the colors and the glittery essence of the big *Ka-boom!*, that woman would be spastically grasping at the air and pulling in the memories of such an explosion, never before seen by her and hopefully, never to be seen again. She would know that it holds relevance and meaning, but how does one encapsulate meaning into an interesting tale of deliverance? It has to have enough substance to engage the reader and keep them interested. It would have to pack a punch, yet not offend too much. It would have to consist of just the right amount of tenderness, affection, loss and dismay – but with enough understanding to make a play for the heart strings of everyone who could identify and God knows there's a bunch of them.

And then there's the timeline. Do I take it back to the early-birth-quack-social-worker-from-Stone-Ridge timeline that she thought she was professional enough to give an opinion on, but which she failed miserably? Or just start at day one of "Once Upon a Time: The Uncut Version"? Heh. The uncut version could sometimes be recalled as more of a mini-series or marital encyclopedia of what not to do when betrothed. Purposeful though; I do believe that it was all purposeful.

Well, until my firework thoughts calm enough to rub the particles out of my eyes and tackle this project head-on, I'll put out there to ask that you stay-tuned. This is going to evolve, I can tell!

Thursday, August 12, 2010

Breathing: The Temporary Depletion of Oxygen

It really came as no surprise that my mind once again tricked me into thinking the idealism I harbor was capable of overcompensating for the realism that exists.

There are times when I feel as if I am a spectator to my own life, and how odd a feeling to be routing from the bleachers…for myself. The parameters of human magnificence again I suppose. I'm that rat in the maze of legal blunders. Right turn; left turn then a circle-'round, then *Bam*…I run smack-dab into a petition, or a summons, continuing litigation and most certainly, notice of charge for a $50 phone conversation that I don't recall having.

When I read, I come across the bravest of statements to take charge, take control and become accustomed to the good things happening when you're able to drop the negativity at the door and welcome the breadth of change with open arms. On certain days, this rainbow outlook is more difficult to maintain than others. Today = certain day. Why is that? The evolution of everything; it's everywhere. It's like the quote: "The more things change, the more they stay the same" we somehow become accustomed to change that's really not. The flipside of this, of course is that we could choose to be the change. Where in essence, we're the ones making the change. I question if this is always a safe thing to do; probably not. I remember pushing pretty hard a number of years ago in order to make something happen – something that I thought I was in desperate need of having happened and when all was said and done — well, here I am, longing to get out.

Deep breath. (Did you know that there's an actual technique to proper breathing? Yeah, who knew?) Apparently, I've been screwing up the breathing pattern and thereby, losing vital amounts of oxygen in the process. Guess that explains why some days go bye in a zinger and others are mellow atonement of the exercise of inhale/exhale. Either way, there's purpose in them there walls and here I've been with my pick-ax, fumigating mask and galoshes, hoping that it'll all collapse before I do. Take another step toward the purpose of creating the life I see and have faith. That's where the context of it all lies.

Okay — for the sake of life as I know it, I'll work on my breathing patterns and this exhausting exercise in futility. I'll be certain to say my prayers at the dinner table and before bed....and when I brush my teeth in the morning and at work....oh, and during my breaks, and when I'm weeding the garden and when I'm in the bathroom....

You get the point.

You Don't Know What You're Doing

Language:

That elusive pet that we each engage in the morning; that irritating reminder that we sometimes don't measure up, language is the vehicle for all thought, action and intention.

I often wear my heart on my sleeve, I'm entirely too sensitive at times and succumb to bouts of depression when I'm not cognizant of where my head is at. I take more than my share of things personally and as if they're an attack on my heart. I often can't explain what I'm thinking because there simply seems to be too many words and one, in particular…that I'm thinking of as the main descriptor.

On many occasions this is a "flaw" so-to-speak of the Type-A personalities and often, one of the most difficult issues to compete with. I've sat countless hours in therapeutic seminars and stress-relief classes where I've felt the need to correct the speaker or have inserted my own set of verbiage in order to clear the air for the way I could feel my mind processing what I was hearing. This…Is not a good thing.

This morning, the thought occurred to me that there is a power given to language depending on the context, form and tone of the message; mostly tone. When handed an insult, it becomes insulting depending on the way that we perceive our own self image. If someone were to call a name that has no meaning in our mental dictionary that word would then cease to have any power. On the other hand if someone insulted our ability to be a "good" person, a "great mom", or the way that we look – reacting as if an insult is in a sense, to say that we have agreed with enough of the statement to feel powerless against it. That we additionally think we're not "as good" a person as we should be/ could be, that we're not a "great" mom, that we are: 'ugly, stupid, ignorant, etc.' enough so, that hearing the statement from someone else is as if they're exposing our vulnerabilities to everyone…and how dare they!

It's probably the reasoning behind why I have such a difficult time developing a resume. Whoever played with the chemistry set for making a ME must have eye-balled the recipe and put in way too much idealism because I find it very difficult to fib about having the ability to do things or be something that I don't feel 100% about doing or being. You know, cutting and pasting in all those action words and power phrases for grabbing the attention of a prospective employer: managed, detailed, organized, lead, prioritized, supervised, and so forth. It never seems to measure up to enough of a description for my real abilities and always lacks in what I'm intending to present as a one-page descriptor of my self. And while we're on the subject, who ever said that resumes should only be one page? I've read enough of the self-help resume starter kits for creating something fabulous to know that it should be original and spectacular like an action thriller movie trailer, but yet be in compliance with margin settings, highlighted name and contact information, font size and be in Times New Roman style. Dumb. Whenever I get to step 4 of the "create your own masterpiece resume", I indefinitely quit because my urge is rather to scrap steps 1 through 4 and start over with a poster board, some finger paints and a medley of candid pictures, a sharpie marker, those shape-cutting scissors and a glue stick. I'd fill little comic bubbles with quotations from past employers and coworkers and then sum it all up with a highlighted statement (in much larger font) from someone prestigious that I'd cunningly convince to speak as to my abilities and standards. None of it would be a lie, so I wouldn't be stumbling over what to write where and how to phrase the statements, yet stay in the lines of what constitutes a proper representation of me. And it would be catchy, brightly colored and give the reader a face to identify with a quirky, glittery past because of all my candid shots.

Back to the original message however, language is the problem. It's the drive and the roadblock – and how much of a conundrum that something can exist two-fold like that. The root cause of all internal battling, at least on my count it is.

"You don't know what you're doing…"

"Yes I do! No, actually I don't. Wait. What did you say? What am I doing? I know! I know what to do!"

From the perspective that language is a mirror being held to our faces, or more appropriately, that insulting language is a mirror – that it can enable us to identify our problem areas…well, that's much more pleasing that it being a constraint restraint to our delicate psyche. It's like being a student rather than everyone else always being our jailor. So the next time I catch a phrase of "you don't know what you're doing…" I can mentally respond with the: "You know what? No. I don't. Gotta work on that." And then go about whatever it was that I didn't know I was doing. Inevitably, it all works out in the end anyway, so vehicle or not, language is the voice-over for life. Heh. And to think that all I wanted to know is why resumes have to be limited to one page?

Mental

She came to suggest it was a manifestation of the mind.

That's the only way she would be able to validate everything that had gone down over five years. How uniformly the pieces lined up too, when she uttered the words: "only in my head". To herself of course, there were very tangible issues occurring succinctly with those that played in her psyche. They were different though; the tangible ones. They were the ones that had places, times, patterns and cut far deeper than the reasoning assigned by apologies. They scarred over but were picked at by the mental pick-lock kit and they'd even heal if only she'd stop tonguing the thoughts; the blame.

Between what she could see and feel and that which she could not, she hovered. Determined not to role-play the victim any longer gave a fierce blow of freedom and power, but also engaged the mental minions of doubt and fear to engage the wheels of uncertainty. And yet - she recalled how determination had led her to this very place where she now beckoned it to take her from. Faulty wiring, maybe. She did allow for enough time to pass until deciding upon the cognitive reproach after all. If there was something else that might explain all this, then maybe it would venture to be heard before running off. Yes? Yes? No.

In her mind's eye she could see that charred treasure map that was the layout of her life. The destination, always being happiness, was fraught with heartache and hardship when she backed up her game piece from the space it resided. She'd gone too far ahead on the board before paying the jailer or having that audit done. And quite simply; that was not allowed.

Mental; it was all mental.

Casper Was A Punk

He (why was Casper a "he" anyway? It's not as if he had any organs to differentiate his sex, right?) had no cause to existing as a fathom of one's imagination, he just hovers around, poking at whatever insecurities might exist when the lights are all turned out. Some threads of our existence quest for identifying the ghosts, I think. To have a tangible thought to assign our fears to maybe. Or that we can generate hypertension in lieu of contending with the real change agents of character.

Change agents are really the masquerading "Casper's" - the chubby, rounded, smiling and floating fear-driven punk that's invading individual progress. The flip side of this though is that the little apparition is as transparent as breath in wintertime.

Take the change agents, the ghosts, the fears as a tool, ... and therein lies real growth. Too afraid of being presented with what's on the other side of Door Number 1...or 2...or...it is typical; comfortable to stay with what we know. In that however, everything else additionally stays the same. A comfortable numbness might show face at this stage, often accompanied by depression, psychotropic medication and eventually, the withering of our core, until we're so mechanical that we don't challenge any longer. The Casper's of the psyche won't give any indication that blunt survival (if you can title it that..."survival") is the end goal of initiating fear, but it is. Those who don't challenge, don't pose a problem. Or as an attorney once presented to me, "just take your sour grapes and go home"; a "don't question my authority!" expected of the masses.

Getting back to the immensity of change agents, or as I like to see them, the would-be life altering accelerator to potential power. We each have several opportunities throughout life to acknowledge and accept our challenges and venture on into the unknown, flashlight or not. With each step of intention into that unknown we gain strength and a clearer perspective. Not to be paralyzed by those little stormtroopers of ignorance, we should recognize those threads of opportunity, rise to the occasion and swallow hard the idea that your life will never, ever be the same. But you must, must...must, be willing to do the work, put in the time, make the changes that unfold to you, wake up... and breathe. Recognize that the only thing that will stall the process, the awakening, the movement; the only thing that will inhibit growth, or halt awareness is fear. Fear that the recipe might not produce a delicacy, or fear that the end product will render us with less than our start. Fright of a hundred cognitive "what if" scenarios for every small percentage of change we're called to do. And why? Because Casper is a punk!

The Hourglass

February of 2006 delivered a lyrical blow with the release of Cowboy Mouth's Voodoo Shoppe CD. Every note, each word, I swear was targeted at me and if ever I dreamed to purge my emotions of the black-hole voids, it was then. And purge I did! The love of my life (who, I might add is not crazy) stood beside me as I landed stage side, rocking the stones right out of my costume jewelry rings and mutilating the semi-precious metals because of all my beat, beat, beating on the sub-woofers. That concert rocked my soul in early 2006; I was alive!

And now, September 2010 as the summer draws to an end, this surging desire rears again. This time though, with Zac Brown Band's fall release of "You Get What you Give," CD and particularly, the "Let it Go" track. Repeating over and again in my environment, the "let it go" phrase and ideology reverberates through every waking moment and interrupts my subconscious while I sleep. Tonight marking the Autumnal Equinox and a very full moon, I'm prefacing all thought patterns and emotive reactions with the tide receding; finally. It's clear skies ahead and full intention of loosening my grip.

I do feel however, that with the heavy-handed suggestion of "just let go", there should come a warning. Something akin to: "Not as easy as it sounds"; or "Expect a ration of retaliation", or "internal combustion may occur if occupant happens to be a Type-A personality". Something.

Mid-month September marked the New Moon, a phase that I was sure would linger longer with the coming of dreams, the going of nightmares. It seems to have been short-lived given the knock-about I've endured these last two weeks. Though it is suggestible there may be a reasoning there too. I don't know. I was pretty certain that a weekend at a cabin in Vermont with the leaves changing, the smell of apple cider in the air and my best lovey, would cure my heartache, but...

I'm processing.

That's what it is. Processing.

Similar to that little hourglass symbol that comes up on your screen when you're waiting for the next function to take.

Processing.

I did purge again recently, actually am in the process of purging to take it a step further. This here and now involves a conundrum of empathy, memories, intentions and a boat-load of "Yes, but why…" questions. That. Needs to stop. Let it go! Then I recollect – thinking of the times spent in sessions, sitting, waiting, wishing (again, to quote a musician with lyrical mysticism). Sitting, waiting, wishing. And all that time spent in an oversized, stuffed chair with a delicate golden-weave and a fifteen dollar co-pay – well, I thought it counted. Maybe in some sense of the "process" it does count – but right here and now it doesn't feel like that.

I think of the purging as if a vomitorium; in layers. Or a timeline. Peeling back the layers of stuffed baggage, and damage, and …crud, is no easy feat. And I actually enjoy picking through what others might consider "garbage" – that whole trash/treasure idea you know. This one though, aye. This purging situation leaves much to be desired and actually, I think it's given me an ulcer, a headache, and has most-definitely affected my sleep patterns.

So, as long as we're on this musical road to recovery, I'll leave you with the mental picture of Ray Lamontagne's verbiage: "I looked my demons in the eyes, laid bare my chest and said 'Do your best'".

I don't think they have the moxy, to tell the truth.

Memento

There is a delicately planted lipstick kiss mark on the rearview mirror of my truck. It arrived a few weeks ago from a dear friend of mine, who I can just picture as she smacked her kisser together with a nice shade of Burt's Bee Balm and was perfectly poised before planting a reminder for me on what I would have thought was entirely too dirty a surface. In her defense, love knows no boundaries, which applies even to muddy mirrors and parked vehicles.

At this point, the balmy reminder is slightly coagulated and speckled with the remnants of brazen little bugs that dove head on at 65 mph into my memorabilia, only to discover the sticky surface too late. I'm going to leave it there – and what a great token it is.

I'd contemplated a visit to the car wash because the postal delivery lady was kind enough to put one of those nifty 50% off coupons in my mailbox. However, after I did the calculations on my would-be savings, I've decided that my smooch is worth more than the $4.28 credit that I'd have in my bag.

I laughed this morning at the idea of this little muse of mine, jaunting through the side yard and curiously contemplating how she'd leave her mark on my world while I was away. These moments; those actions – come at precisely the right time in a life that sometimes is too rushed to gather your breath from. So little red-headed muse – THANK YOU!

You mean the world to me.

Absolutely; Positively

I am currently finding myself absolutely, positively irritated to the maximum of my being over the issue of absentee-parenting and ignorant-fueled "guidance" (if you can call it that).

It's late.

My little one - the essence of childhood, heads to the bathroom to brush his teeth. Sibling-trickery is the name of the game as he goes about explaining to his older sister why he spread hand soap across the bristles of her toothbrush. There's a hint of laughter in the air as the reasoning makes its way to the excuse.

He says that he always has to deal with soap in his mouth. That he's always being directed to consume a sudsy matter when the stepmother of the West comes into play with her dictatorship antics and lack of good parenting style.

What?!

As he's being reprimanded for the sake of health over concerns that soap will cause sickness to someone he cares about, he's duly-explaining that this kind of thing happens constantly when he's at his dad's house.

Since when is that kind of guardianship allowed to run freely over the land? It's not.

He says he has to do it when he's forgetful. Or when he mistakenly trips down the stairs because, (as she believes) he's not paying attention.

And this woman runs a daycare center?

Oh, to get my common sense in an injection form and inoculate the charge-parties of the county government seat.

In an honest token of biology, it doesn't take more than a misguided effort to create a child — and though that might make one lost soul a "parent", it by no means, makes you a father…or mother.

Take heed, dear stand-in placement of guardian-over-my-child: your concurrent acts of embarrassment and degradation, while your husband remains inattentive, shall be construed as direct and intentional efforts of abuse; not "guidance" as you may conceive them to be.

Likewise, the same establishments which have naively supported your daycare establishment will be noticed by your poor judgment and inadequate, lacking, and immature parenting. And though I understand this may mean nothing to a county which oozes corrupted policy, you surely comprehend that it means worldly-measures to a woman that simply does. not. give. up.

Absolutely, positively,

Me

Why is precisely the reason.

Why? Because it is fun. Because it brings laughter, enjoyment and wedge of memory that will not dislodge.

Why?

Because there are too many reasons why not. That is why.

There was a time when I thought that in order to perfect the art of planning, one had to immerse themselves in some delicate field of professionalism that gave enough weight to their purpose to justify the end result.

Not so.

After boiling down the crude ingredients of what it means to be human; to learn and live and wonder...and wander, there is so much more able to be said about the unanswerable "why?" then there is to be explained by the "because".

Just live.

Let it be.

Enjoy. And dammit, hold on for the ride with the most zealous hairspray in your bouffant and the zestiest of nail polish colors on your digits. Do not fear the answering of "why?" — live it. And when you do decide to unbuckle to let the next rider board, smile a smile that says "Brotha, it's worth it — but I give you no more than that" and make sure that smile spreads from ear to ear.

When all is said and done, it is for the mere pleasure of the ride, not the safety restraints or the approval received beforehand.

Breaking out the rule book, solely for the intention of burning it as soon as the burn-ban is lifted. Or before...before would be alright too.

Wham! Bam!

The Hardest Wall

A hair's breadth from Christmas and the air is still. There is something that lingers, untold truths, begotten lies that fill the space between right and wrong. It never comes easy to stand on faith alone but that is where we reside. The effort at mental creation of black and white has long since dissipated in this stale and stagnant environment. Try as we may — it feels harder to gather the energy to remain calm and present the facts as they stand, hoping someone will listen.

I wonder why? Why is it that what presents as evil, manipulative and coercive is more easily accepted, welcomed almost, than the truth? What has brought us to the brink of extinction among ourselves? I know I didn't start out this way, but yet, here I am. Wondering...

Unsettled with what my mind returns to me as an answer.

Attempts to reason with the unreasonable fumble the hope and I watch it wobble across a field that a growing part of me doesn't believe in. To justify this feeling would be to suggest that once again, the essence of life must be fortified in faith. That one small and tender offshoot of a larger, and dying mainstay.

Faith don't fail us now.

Just Thinking

I feel that I have given more than enough thought to this. It circulates around the fact that I am semi (emphasize "semi") sorry that you are in fact, lame. There is not quite enough emphasis in your language to justify giving thoughts of you another go-'round and there is definitely not enough justification to allow your words to breathe any longer than the air they encompass when passing through your lips.

That's not all.

You are, in fact, wrong. You do not care as deeply as a mother should. And arrogance does not compensate for immaturity. Nevertheless, it is not my place to pass judgment, so I am simply stating my perspective and shall leave it as such until someone else is willing to validate the truth that I see and speak.

On a day that one is willing and able to be as much of a strong person as one verbosely claims, then ...and only then, will I listen contently and move accordingly. That. Has not happened so far.

I stand on accounting to one motivation only - that is truth. Truth, (not to be confused with truth) shall set you free and in as much as I would like to assist, I cannot. Truth can only be found through long-plodding, and sometimes sorrowful efforts as a seeker. truth, on the other hand, is often confused with and linguistically challenged by the commonalities that bind mankind. (I personally feel it is the capital "T" that does it in).

Evermore,

and with much anticipation,

Selflessness-in-measure-yet-slightly-perturbed,

Me

Friday, December 24, 2010

Resolution Solution

I, _____ do hereby resolve:

- To no longer be bound by critical overviews, self-serving perspectives or ego-filled commandments. They are not mine, I shall not harbor or accept them

- To act in the sole interests of safety and well-being for my self, my children and my family and to negate all other efforts of control by parties unaligned to this objective, with the strength of faith over explanation

- To be a seeker of truth and be cognizant that there are times when what I may want may not coincide with what I need – and greater still, that it is not I who is in charge

- To ask for help and be unafraid of receiving it

- To place greater belief in the challenges that are placed before me that they will make me great

- To say "thank you" more than I have expectations

- To lose expectations, or rather, replace them with anticipations and preparations for the glories that will undoubtedly be bestowed upon my life

- To hone my focus on forgiveness

- To pray for contentment over understanding, explanation of, or worry

- To return the smile lines to my face, dirt to my fingers, sunshine to my shoulders, and blue paint to my toenails

- To engage in more random acts of kindness

- To journal and pen letters more than I document wrong-doings

- To dissolve anger, hatred, and jealousy to the grit of sandy beaches – that it will be washed away not by me, but by time and the act of being forgiven

- Above all, I resolve to accept that where I now stand, what air I now breathe, and the placement that I now exist in is precisely where I am supposed to be

Signed, this 24th day of December, 2010 with much Faith, determination and God as my witness,

_____

Put My Finger On It

Dear Lacking Self-Esteem and Void of Security,

You bring me nothing but problems.

I'm leaving you.

Don't call.

It Was Not Plainly Clear

Of course, it often isn't plainly clear. Moreso, it comes across as paralleling a bad night in Mexico with some persons that are not. so. trusty.

I happened upon the scene with a lofty head filled with idealism and a mouth wrought for writing...or speaking. Wrought for speaking; wait, no writing. At least that is what I had been told by persons not so wrought. Personally, I didn't see it. It was a combination of being blinded by the light (as my buddy Bruce dost protest) and a labor of love that would, might, possibly, eventually enable me to be a better person capable of transient work and bestowed efforts of the family context that I so desired.

I was hopeful.

Hopeful bites sometimes. A lot of sometimes, sometimes.

The point was to gain enough experience as a person, an advocate, a mother, speaker-of-truth, and outright human being, that I would gain enough strength points to move to the next level. Truth be told, I often used cheat codes and moved along passively because I thought I'd mastered the lamest of elements only to find that I was the lamest and would be moving back several spaces until I conceded to run due course. Phewy.

A side note of suggestion offers that I have mentally compiled a resolution list of ideas toward my next role: Awesomeness. I have a book-signing (equipped with author-signed pages of my first and best-selling novel; currently untitled and missing each page beyond that there signed page), a children's book of characters who parallel the life and times of me and my son (and Lovey — Lovey's always there!), and the perfect act and wording for when I am let go due to budget constraints. Seems profitable, right?

Ought to.

This has taken me a lot of years to compile.

Where now? That is the point at which I currently reside. It is either continue down the road of least-resistance/no achievement and no forward-movement for the sake of being "easy" — OR a big, fat: double-barrel bustin' truth on the situation, eat-my-grits, bite my dust and go big, or go home kind of circumstance.

Big, fat?

Yeah. I'm leaning in that general direction too.

I find a large issue with the legal society that happens to run, organize and fund much of society. WHEN the heck did that happen?!?! And why wasn't I invited? Doesn't seem right. Isn't right.

But...

I have had this pot on the stove for far too long, finally turned the heat up and have a reduction of fine, unadulterated comprehension that will pair nicely with a baguette and the "No BS clause" that I put at the opposite end of that book-signing deal where all I have is a cover page. (I guess that isn't entirely true — I have the No BS clause as well).

She

She was amazing.

She was innocent and uninhibited. She spanned the time from dawn to dusk; never realizing that it mattered.

She encompassed the entirety of true, unadulterated love and compassion toward that which brought her happiness.

Her happiness is him.

He knows that. She reminds him as much as that delicacy allows and pushes the limits of mushy, smushyness that would make grown men bashful and red in the face. She doesn't care though.

It is important to tell; to talk about and be reminiscent of. That is what she believes anyway. She is currently in the process of comparing her romanticism to the novels of Shakespeare and love that cannot be compared to.

Carrying on with the wings of a cupid (minus the semi-nakedness).

Ahhhh, love.

The Buck Stops Here

By my calculations (and mind you, I have had to learn a quite irresponsible way of calculating this scenario) this situation is as precisely screwed up as it is allowed to be. I walk in with a semi-smug grin upon my face thinking that maybe for once, the truth shall set the situation free.

No dice.

Stupid dice.

Whoever signed me up for this game anyway?

Be that as it may, in the case that one might not be completely accustomed to small claims court - let me shed some light:

They care not so much about the issues that you bring legally, but the best defense offered by a skater-brained dimwit on the opposing side who happens to have the much desired ESQ behind the initials of her name. ESQ mind you, means little more than "extremely & stupidly qualified" to speak...I digress...

I defend myself. I do blush a tad and skip a word here and there, but hey! I'm a layman. Give. Break. Jerk. And besides, Esq didn't defend honestly anyway. She blathered on about inconsequential numbers that she read directly from an order that was A: old, and B: illegitimate (and we're all about illegitimacy here I thought, no?)

In addition, and to be completely fair, one such person in position of judgeship stated that he did not care to (and I paraphrase) "address a situation which was clearly a debacle of mass proportions - ergh, dismissed without prejudice...sorry lady, take it back to the party that has done NOTHING for you for five years and counting. Good day."

I'm striking on the court system!

Join if you feel ye are capable of holding one such sandwich board large enough to discuss such lunatic rantings as I feel the need to rant.

On a sunnier day I might consider this to be part and parcel with the matters of divorce, but at five years - this crap is getting old, and curdling my blood. Besides that, I swear I have a new set of divinely inscribed crow's feet upon my forehead. (Did I mention "strike"?).

Eh. I consider this a fallacy and will call this week a "week" to the capacity that my vocabulary allows with children in the room (they don't need to hear my real feelings). And tomorrow...tomorrow, I will consider myself lucky if I don't rack up a charge or two.

I get it though, I really do. One court has the extension of their legal arms, criminally speaking - which goes only so far as public housing issues and that of the stereo-typed baby-daddy's crowding Main Street, but C'MON! You can't exert power as legal ramification upon a man so delusionally human as to help a woman out?! What happened to the foundation of this place anyway? They all leave or something? The only answer that we conjure is to return to a place which has obviously accomplished squat in half a decade that would, might, probably should on a highly-medicated day have me believing that they will do something?

Malarkey.

Monark Files: I

(Originally published September 2008)

The Monark Files - I:

We step lightly into a classroom painted to the ceilings with characters from the well-known Sponge-Bob cartoon. Hefty mothers, all toting large egos, condescending questions and dragging their frightened children behind them, step on my toes with eagerness to be the first in line, the first with a question and the first of recognized mothers in this liberal setting East of Home. Granting them to pass before me and my son, they quickly find their child's seat and plop them in it with a fierceness; moving on to ask Ms. Teacher stupid questions about reminding little Johnny that he has to go 2 and can ask for assistance in wiping his behind. My eyes scan the room as I hold firmly to the belief that this is somewhat backwards, irritable and nothing less than wrong. I feel G's little grip on my hand and as it tightens, look down to see his knuckles turning white. He looks up at me with a question of what to do next? I look around the room for the little miniature of a school scenario that might behold the name of my dear child – and my eyes fall upon the display for butterflies that is no doubt posted with pride. Four inch letters spanning the top of this monstrous, artistic display shows clearly the aptitude for our new venture – there it is: M-O-N-A-R-K Butterflies. MONARK? Really?

Of all that is semi-precious and eluding – you can't get the name right? The English right? The grammar? The First Impression? Oh Heavenly days, what has happened to the trademark of profession? Of pride in leadership, and of recognizing your faults and CORRECTING them? I suppose it goes hand in hand with the fact that Ms. Teacher kept referring to my son as "Colin" – and on correction, she told me "That's your son!" I allowed her to be enlightened as to the fact that seeing as how I participated in the naming of such a child, I would know his name and it was. Not. Colin. Anyway, it has brought new light to the case-scenario of being assigned this grab-bag of a school system. All things come to light with enough patience – in the meantime, I think that I'll join the PTA. Take a controlling stance on what's circling the school about me.

The Act of Being a Bieber
(July 2008)

They catch a lot of slack, those Bieber's.

I'm one of them and not until recently, have I realized the full extent of what it actually means to be of such blood. I've held tight to the reigns of spiritual rationalization and the effects of good karma, but being of the Bieber lineage really adds a touch of class to the situation, and my growing comprehension of it makes for a new perspective.

Eight children into the world of family allowed for my Mother and Father to prime a small farming town for what would become the largest onslaught of truth and morals this side of the Canadian border. It was wondrous - having the responsibility of walking a fine line of truth while the remainder of those you met, fell by the wayside of pressures and defeat. I'm no Mother Mary, and Lord knows I've made my fair share of wrong decisions (for which I'm indebted to) but the realization that eventually makes its way into adulthood, adds another twist. You see, being a Bieber isn't just another notch in the totem pole, it's a history. You're born into morale, family, understanding, hard-core heritage and ethics. You can sway from side to side while prancing through the teenage/young adult years, but inevitably, you return to the foundation of those morals and build (again, if necessary) from there. You have the foundation, and so, it cannot be trampled upon.

Review the past six years or so and you'll find (at least in my scenario) that the Bieber name has been spat on, squatted over and looked down upon, but it remains steadfast against the mouths of those treacherous liars - and all with a smile. For there is truth in a smile - and that's the ingredient that can't (in most situations) be handled.

We entered this week with the knowledge that my little boy's going to be five soon. He's skipping around his childhood with all too much responsibility on him already, but he does it with a humbleness that only God can grant. I check the calendar and because we dance with every-other weekend through our year, I figure that the weekend of his birthday, he won't be here so what better to do than have an early birthday party? One that's really special - one that's family. Afterall, he's part of the Bieber family and what better to offer than that? So we pack our bags, our new bike for G. and head West. Walking in the door late at night, was when it hit me. The light was left on for our arrival as my Mother always said that it's "so unwelcoming to come home to a dark house", so the light above the countertop flickers with content waiting for the birthday boy.

The room is ready - beds for the kids, the smell of being home circulating around the house and just enough of a breeze to remember that it's Summertime and oh, so beautiful. I hear the laughter from my brother and sister, who've waited up all night for us to visit, as they're sitting in the room watching reruns of Daffy Duck. Just as I'm signing out for the night, the rest of my family says their "hello's" and their "goodnights" and diverge to bedrooms that have the quilts of generations-past on the beds and hugs for the promise of tomorrow in the evening. They're tired - tired from the hard work that makes up each day - but it's a good tired. A "thank God I'm alive" tired and you see that in every smile. It's a "we wish we could help more" tired and a "I have something wonderful to show you in the morning" tired, and I miss it!

The following two days were glorious with my newly polished love - it's watching my children take part in what is the most amazing part of my life; being a Bieber. They long for it, just as I do - they see that it takes hard work, sweat and tears to build a family such as mine and they want in. I want to give them an in - well, really they're already there. I guess it's the outside pressures - those termites of family values that are trying to eat their way through the structure. Damn things don't realize that we're all immune. Immunity because of Faith, and Belief, and Trust. The termite infestation is like being bitten by a mosquito after you've sprayed on the Spring Fresh Bug spray, wondering "how do they know to bite me?" Faith, belief and trust give you Truth - which is precisely the ingredient that will be the downfall. Like the pillars of salt - they'll erode. I suppose I'm wishing that they'd erode at a bit faster pace and at the same time, knowing that I shouldn't wish such things. Initiate Faith.

It all comes back around, that's what I keep telling myself. Just as my understanding for my wonderful family has highlighted the toils and tribulations - it's the essence of being part of something truly extraordinary and waking up to find yourself smack, dab in the middle of it all. It'll come back around. For now, I'm thinking that there must be some way to sell tickets or give out "family favors" or something - maybe a billboard...

Breakfast on Sunday summed up the entire weekend. We sit around the family dinner table - all totaling sixteen and out of the mouths of babes, comes, "I'm a Bieber!" The smiles from fifteen other faces made my heart glad.

Blimey
(Originally Published April 2008)

And so, I'm waiting.

Don't know how this has all contorted itself to a HUGE snake-like masquerader, but it most-certainly has become such.

I wish for the life of me that I could return to a time when things weren't troublesome and life-sucking.

What is that, a succubus? I know by definition it's the form of a woman - well, in this case it would be that of a man. No, boy...no... testosterone-induced being. Rage and conspiracy have taken the seat of what used to be a vile attempt at truth. That poser!

(*This is your mind speaking*) "Move along; move along already."

I'm trying to! What is it that keeps the bindings so damn tight? There's no blood coursing through my veins anymore - more like sewer sludge. Urgh.

Point?

Don't have any other way to say it: "Stop using my little boy as fodder for your games!" I didn't place possessive terms on him before, but dammit - this time around it's a new ball game.

You don't give a shit, so be it...go pollute someone else. I'm tired of playing.

Thank You
(Originally Published August 2007)

You know when you reach a point that all the thinking in the world won't undo itself. It's created a place in your mind that nearly reaches form and function. They're just thoughts though, how does that happen? Either way, these "formed" thoughts are like a little ball-bearing that rolls itself, independently powered, from side to side in that head of yours.

With the process of thinking such thoughts, I actually made some headway this time and figured it out. Here I've been asking the universe for things, crying out to the night with wonder of why I had not been blessed with at least a sampling of the dreams that were torn down some time ago? Never reaching the end of that thought process to realize that I had, indeed, been blessed with more than I could imagine.

Teaching; an aspiration of mine that was placed on the back burner.

Family; that's a big one...full and rounded this idea of family, children, spouse, and any other individual that may need a spot of soup and pat on the back - that's what would complete my idea of family. I wanted it for myself - to love and care for and create a "home" with, residing on the other burner in the back.

A house; this one not so much the actual style and design of a house, but rather, this was more highly concentrated on the functionality of a house. It needs to be grand - light pouring in from all the windows, scrolled metal works on the walls, art hanging in the entry-way to welcome any and all inside the beautifully crafted doors. It needs to be open - the energy of the rooms, the floor plans crafted in such a way as to create a natural path for little feet in the night, creeping to my bedroom for snuggies. It needs to be strong - sometimes a necessity to compensate for my lack in strength, but more for the solidarity of the ages that it shall experience. A vase, yes...that's it. It's function would be most like that of a vase, capturing the stories, the warmth, the laughter and the legends of a thousand tales.

Anyway, here I thought that I allowed someone to destroy all of that for me. I was sulking; really, I was. I've been somewhat of a hermit, rationalizing my actions and wondering of the rest that I see. If the universe had the potential to smack me upside the head, I believe it would have happened several times already. Regardless, I reached my "Aha!"

The teacher: I have five children in my home to teach. Their ages, their experiences and their history - all perfect tools for a teacher because they are so eager to learn. Ready to learn the best of what there is to learn - about people, relationships, family, loving others, optimism, being strong, standing firm...on and on the list goes.

The Family: I was gifted an instant family by loving their father. This man, I don't speak of often enough because I've been so wrapped around and tormented by the idea of a psychotic-episodic marriage.

Really though, Chris, you're worth more than the words can relay. As a father, friend, lover, spouse, confidant, partner, mate, teacher... you've done a fantastic job at all of these. Because of your faithfulness, I believe I'm seeing the forest from the trees this time. We really do have a wonderful family.

And the home: that's just another piece of the puzzle. It's created wherever we are - where we are together. The friends, they come and go - and I would hope that they know they are welcome, always. It's there, all these things that I thought I'd lost - I have, in fact, found them and they were right in front of me all along.

So to you, Chris, thank you. Thank you for your patience and understanding. Thank you for being in control - for never harming us, me, the kids. Thank you for not running away even if I said I wanted to. For being compassionate, even when I was in uber-witch mode - for trying, always trying. Thank you most for being a real father to your children. It's an achievement in and of itself, as the persons that step up to the plate to take care of one child, much less more than one child, are few and far between. And with that - thank you for showing a little boy what it really means to be a dad. You've done it and you've done a superb job. Thank you for loving us; me and the kids. Thank you.

Muy Importante

I feel the need to say that because there is a large part of your humanity lacking, and because our son has been filled to the brim with the fear placed upon him should he actually express his true wishes in your general direction...and because, well, honestly, I'm sick to death of your ignorant games - you should seriously consider a new hobby. One that consists of yourself in a small room, no windows, many sharp objects and ... I'll stop.

Okay, blessings in your direction.

Honestly though, you need to stop~!

Our child has been through enough. So much so that he is beginning to decipher this ridiculousness for himself and for your sake, I don't like what I see. I try my hardest to convince him that the end is worth the effort where it concerns you, but more times than not — it's hard for me to see as well. After five years of litigation, and an additional five years of marital what's-it-called, I am tired of covering tracks. Basically, a decade of learning has produced one such woman not willing to produce bullshit for an arrogant, egotistical, and belly-aching belligerent fool that shows no thankfulness. Even more...

As it stands, our child expresses (with the full use of his extensive vocabulary) that he does not wish to see you on this coming Monday because of the disgracing menagerie of antics you will put him through. I will call on Saturday. I will call on Sunday. Each day a day unto itself, I pray will produce some reaction from our child that enables me to believe you have not coerced him and I will take appropriate action at that time.

Sadly, your irresponsibility makes me ill.

Nothing new. But something in dire need of alteration.

Regards,

The Mother

As If

As if you might understand the dire need to grow beyond your obviously, very small-minded and self-inflicted painful experience as a human, I implore you to speak in a manner more becoming to a woman.

I beseech you to conduct yourself, not as a child like your own...but as an adult. If you want for better, if you wish for greater and dream for more - than pursue it. Don't drown it. Don't let it be drowned. If I offer anything, I present myself as an example of what you will undoubtedly have to contend with in your very near future. It will not get better. It will not get easier. It will only become all consuming, all encompassing and before you realize what has happened, you'll find yourself standing at a broken mirror, wondering why that childhood ideology of yourself as Cinderella has become so tortured and twisted when all you sought at the onset of this relationship you find yourself in, was love and understanding.

Your hair will be thinned and your eyes darkened with drags of skin that hang beneath them. If you have not committed yourself before this point, you will most-likely be so confused with the life and vitality you once had will be all but depleted and your children will sigh heavily with the anxiousness that you spread throughout your house daily. There will be no one who listens any longer, no one who fully understands and no one that cares to join you on your umpteenth episode of martyrdom. If I had to guess, I would put money down that there will come a day (in your situation, I will hope that be sooner, rather than later) that your realization will slam into your consciousness like contact between a freight train and a concrete wall.

Be that as it may, I would advise you to save your energies.

And now that I have allowed an ample amount of time for my previous words to sink in; I agree with my notion. I am sorry for you only to the point that this will be more difficult than you now believe and having lived the torturous relationship between idealism and realism - I can expunge your actions only when you begin showing signs of growth and a want for better.

Until that point - I suppose only time will tell.

Bound and Re-Bound

The day could be described as a metacognitive hostage situation which would not allow her to loosen the bindings around the mental record repeating track 07: "what if...what if...what if...what if...what if..." .

Intervention stepped in somewhere 'round midday and suggested she turn it off. However, that was violently interrupted by immaturity from the audience and jiminy-cricket hanging out on her left shoulder.

Besides, the last diagnosis she had received was something residing somewhere between: "No" and "That's Impossible"...so she wasn't listening much anyway.

You'll have that.

Part I

Eleanor Rootes had a way of speaking to me that made me want to vomit. A dark and callous cloud followed her into a room and left the air lifeless, cold, and depressed. It left me depressed.

It is my professional human opinion that she disgraces the field of law and that of humanity, while we're on the subject. Loose, shriveled folds of skin hang around a leathery neck that hacks a hairball every thirteenth word or so. Her Pomeranian counterpart, the only dreaded beast that would keep company with such a void, had an ironically similar hair-do and touted it in a likeness to its owner. I believe that it is the arrogance; the talking-down to you that she does even though her Esq. has not filled much beyond three, typically size-12 font spaces at the end of her name. Certainly, it has not assisted her clients.

See Eleanor Rootes was the unfortunate assignment of a law-guardian for my son at a time when he was barely off of breast milk. Given the status of what qualifies as "normal" these days, that could be quite disconcerting. For the record: my son was one year old. At our first introduction, she graced my downstairs apartment kitchen with her yellow pad, shaking off the outside and not closing the door behind her. Never the mind, I introduced her to my son, who sat with a full hamburger - all the fixin's, a side of broccoli florets, and a sippy cup spread across his high-chair tray.

The Ties That Bind

It originated as a thought; without plan, without procedure or precedence. In form it made sense, but in function it was quite lacking. Effortlessly really — she approached it effortlessly because that is what love demands.

In no less than a few years, she began to see there was a large, overflowing capacity for him to act outside what normal realms were and do all that he wished without worry for what pain or heartache it might cause. In many ways, that is what drove her to do the things she did. Deciding that no longer would she accept pain, heartache, abuse or atrocities of another put upon her or her child. Somehow that was a problem. People, in general, do not long for resolution when they are enamored with fighting.

How ignorant.

He was ignorant. Still is. Every effort of resolution, of finding a common ground in the middle is put out the door as if a dog who has messed the rug. And not even with that much foreknowledge. He just fights to fight. I think it is because there is a shred of hatred among a serious void of humanity. Either way, it is directed at me. I don't care so much as I worry.

I hate that I talk and it is discounted. I disdain the thoughts of this horrible, rotten, no good, very bad cycle. It makes no difference to those that abuse precisely because they lack the emotion to care. All is said and done and I look like the problem when all I have ever done, ever...is to protect and support my child. Can they say the same?

No.

But not because they don't try to say they are caring - rather, because they're incapable of applying any feeling toward the same cause. Posers of the grandest order. One shred, one element of deceptiveness five years ago, took precedence over truth because some judge in some county might have been having a bad day. I remember that day — I begged and pleaded for resolution; for acknowledgment. They smiled back with that faux pas that shouted: "Shut up you mimicry of a mother because we know you're going to make our job harder". Then passed the gavel to the left for the sake of easing their workload.

What a joke.

Irritating and debilitating joke.

Has me seriously considering the alternative. What is the alternative? To shout louder, to speak more directly and not care of the responsiveness, no matter how ignorantly it is displayed.

Should take pictures.

And record the event.

Except they took my recorder.

Hope

You step a little lighter when you have hope.

I am fondly rekindling elements that made great sense, had strength of faith and the fortitude to outlast the dregs of fog I feel we are finally wiping from our view; siphoning from our heads. I watch my son, my children. Their eyes are light, their hearts, though sometimes debilitated by an angry web of anger and confusion, are open. My son walks with such pride and comfort when he is sure of himself, when he has been reassured that he is doing the right thing. Passing through pictures, I am again taken aback by how quickly time passes when you are not looking; how slowly it goes when you are.

For such a long time, which left as if only a breath, we waited. We have prayed through many a long night and worried lines onto our faces. Even so - the one answer that we longed for never seemed to come. In stages, it appeared - wildly rearing its head only long enough to be a reminder to stay the course. And maybe this road does not end abruptly either, but the efforts of faith have been renewed because we have hope once again.

Grandeur. That is where my contemplating mind circles. That this story is by no means, over. And just when we thought we had figured out its mastery, we have been humbled to understand once again, that we are not in charge.

In my eyes of hopeful merriment, I am ever grateful for having been the recipient of a person who partners every hope, prayer and dream that I have. He, as I, is not presuming to be anything more than our humanity allows, but for this lifetime with me, he is perfect.

To Query

In many ways my mind is on pause and refuses to seek sunshine over inquiry. I coax and offer assistance - somewhat elusive to the quest I am on. Still, it is query that my cognition always filters through all the netting. Webbing really, it is webbing - not netting. Webs that have become so tangled in and amongst themselves that the clarity has long since gone and what remains is like a nest for anger, ego, control, ...the like.

The test, as it seems - is to continue on without the significance of knowing how I will get to my destination.

My broken dream needs mending once again.

The day began in a "sun's coming up later" kinda way. Sick little boy in the house who I had counted the minutes between coughs for the duration of eight and a half hours that he slept. By 9:22pm the night before, we were at every minute to minute and a half. 9:22pm was the last cough for quite a while. I guess the medicine had set in by that time. Poor little one. I tucked the blanket in around his neck and covered those little feet that hung out from below - hoping that he would be able to glean some rest from a very restless evening. The day following would be hard and we both knew that, though no one spoke it outloud.

The idea is to keep it from being spoken as long as we possibly can. So as to not invest any power or authority into the rantings of a lunatic that some of us (him) need to call "Dad". It doesn't always work out that way though. Often, I am as aware as he of the impending ridiculousness that seems to encompass our days, nights, evenings... every waking hour.

The elements that are most disconcerting are that the other side. The side that is passively protected, irritatingly enabled and ignorantly paraded through the motions of a legal forum. I have been heard to rant, "If I was Secretary of the Press, I would..." and "When I am President, I shall..." insights to personal inspirations - all with a commonality that sends the marauder packing with silence as his only friend. No baggage. No pillaging. And certainly, no speaking to further the propensity of ...just plain stupidity.

Why?

Inquiry begs an answer.

What I Cannot Do

I fail to understand on many days.

As for my responsibilities; what I am charged with supplying...I can do that. I can do the accounting for the entire county because the supporting agencies have employed a population of citizens that struggle with a calculator on a good day. I can also do all the driving to and from Dad's house every single day because Dad cannot, will not, outright refuses, to put our child in a safety seat. (Course, this one's almost outdone itself since the NYS child seat laws extend up to age 8 and July marks that birthday. Five years of non-obligatory conduct and the justifiable answer is: "Mom, you can do this since Dad can't")

I can sit and suck up my $4.11 / gallon gasoline at the rate of my truck idling for fifteen minutes at each of those pick ups/drop offs because Dad decides in his controlling demeanor that either (a) he won't interrupt his television show to assist our son with gathering his things, or the more likely candidate of (b) he decides that I can wait until he's ready to let my son out the door. I can continue juggling hours of second grade homework each night with making dinner, starting laundry, doing dishes, putting clothes away, weeding in the garden and completing my own graduate work, because once again – dad was playing in the ding-weeds, or scheming his next move at alienation. I can write letters to verify that what I have said, I mean and what I mean, I will write to each agency that "forgot" to make updates or changes. I can even and do, pray every waking moment that this is all meant for something. That the language I pass along to my son to make sense of this chaos is all worth it. That good does win out in the end and that there are reasons for everything we encounter. I can dry tears and pretend to be strong a hell of a lot more than I actually am, and wake up the next day to do it again.

What I cannot do – is feed this animal any more. It baffles me to the core, to think that if what I think…what I do, and what I've experienced in the field of seeking justice through and unjustified system is but a trickle in the bucket of it all. I am one case - sitting on the bell-curve of insanity with hope, luck and a touch of "well maybe" in my hands. There needs to be change in a big way and it has to start somewhere solid enough to support the waking moment. I do not feel as though I have that; the change. I do think I am coming to the point of understanding how to start it, but I struggle with the formalities of all the pointless processes that are supposed to give substance to the "we're here to help you" slogans slathered on billboards, court room cork boards and county offices.

They are a lie.

What they should read is: "We are dependent on you being dependent on us. Without you – we would not exist. So thank you for seeking help and assistance; we're counting on you!"

The Blue-Eyed Portals

...they left no room for the rising waters that were an emotional riptide of a volcanic eruption. Playing host to all that I had stuffed and squandered on the act of being strong; the white elephant in the room appeared much too fast for my beleaguered response.

She said this would happen. She said that it would be stuffed for a while, and that depending on the presenting pride, that "while" could take far longer than what the psychological community would consider as "normal".

Apparently, my presenting pride did its very best of a job and stuffed for a good, long time.

Until the weekend approached.

An unexacting time frame and there I was: rendered somewhat helpless and as unsuspecting as the rest of the mini subculture that watched in awe. And this was no awe like, "wow, what a cute kitten" awe, but rather — "holy crap, what's her deal?" awe.

Train. Wreck. Awe.

Damn.

But...five hours and the company of the very best of friends later, and I composed myself enough to walk. At least enough to speak coherently. She said that it was "a breakthrough". I swore it was akin to "lame".

She swore this would be helpful.

I thought it a "moment" and one that I did not wish to replicate any time soon.

She said that it would get better from here on out. That all I need to do is talk.

And you know..for as much as I do talk, for as much as I speak but don't say. I think that I can do this. Talk, I mean. Say what it is that I feel building. Maybe if I start small and unsuspecting it will present in more manageable portions that I can categorize.

...in bite-size pieces that won't choke me when I purge.

Grace

Grace being a scarce commodity, I knocked on the door.

The moments in-between fluttering eyelids left a semblance of balance but no real footing.

Not outside the boundaries of faith anyway.

She visited again. Some three or four years have passed since our last face-to-face and she visited again. Not me -but the lone youth of what it means to have vitality for life, to question and seek understanding. She asked him what he felt, thought, wanted and (of all things) how his Mother was doing. Like she really cares. She doesn't. Incapable probably, but one should not assume.

I would have no difficulty expressing how I truly feel if she were brazen enough to ask me, though I doubt she will.

On certain days I sometimes wonder if I have displaced judgment on her. In fairness, I think there is a steaming heap promised to her direction but it is not for me to dole. The meantime brings a little boy once again confused by the cluster of idiocy the adults in his life bring.

As if they know; as if they understand what they're talking about. My motherly perspective offers a young lad taking the time to line his bottom bunk with all thirty-seven stuffed animals before bedtime - or what he calls "his babies". He says they "want to take care of their Pappa", and with a labor of love, lines them along his pillow - favorites by his shoulders and the bigger, tougher ones at his feet because they're closest to the door.

And there is no problem, right? There is no cause for concern. There must be no issues, no unresolved questions, nothing to warrant an official ad litem doing a job that the quote-unquote ad litem's are supposed to do. I justify his concerns with a soft spoken promise that I do believe him. I verify that he has done nothing wrong and promise that tomorrow will be better for the sake of promise and because Mommies, like Daddies, are supposed to protect.

Not be the danger.

In solitude I comprehend that he is growing with stability, with his own understanding and with a heart that mirrors my own. I can give him a sense of faith, belief, and promise that are not purchased but rather, fostered. I can explain to the best of my ability that there are few things in this world that will hurt more than that of a broken heart and promise never to be the one to do that to him. I cannot promise the same for others too close for comfort.

And after he has drifted off to sleep, I can make sure those thirty-seven babies are lined in their fullest, upright position to protect and love the little boy that means the world to his Mom.

Eleanor Rootes: Part Deuce

On the eve of a total lunar eclipse that promised change, she graced the cracked linoleum floors of the county court. The smell of some state-issued bio-cleanser hung in the air with stale coffee and the beeping sound of a metal detector working too hard. While fumbling with the id-tag hanging 'round her neck on a dingy lanyard, she threw back her tresses that were stuck between collar folds and identification that should have read: "Eleanor Rootes, Law Guardian Sans Litem".

Having the slighted attention of some passing legal commuters, she made what she thought was a clever comment and then turned to find my stare burning holes through her lacking humanity and tanned leather body hide void of intelligent thought. Quickly, she turned away and pretended to be interested in a wall hanging that did not exist.

My name was called among the masses. 9:00 am and I was already being directed to a stagnate eight by five foot cell... er, briefing room. At a stumbling consult with an attorney, rather, "Associate" who has been nonexistent for the two months between adjournments - he questioned what I would like accomplished. I explained that "because I'm pretty, I can do whatever I want". He chuckled without thinking it funny. I had to explain the comprehension with a reminder that the logic of the statement originated with Eleanor. This was her mighty defense at our last go-'round. His eyes bent the way that plastic does when it's heated but still, with no real processing energy available.

How pointless is she?

Very.

They're actually attorneys you know. In the state of New York, law guardians must pass the bar before they aspire to apply to the law guardian panel and be assigned counsel for children through some over-burdened family court. To my knowledge, this particular court has ceased the assignment of cases to her because Eleanor's track record holds too many complaints. And there are the accusations of her dancing beneath the full moon without clothes.

Yes, that happens.

But she's a law guardian charged with proper interpretation of my son's wants, wishes, and desires; proper being the action word.

Eleanor has never set a scraggly foot into our house.

Yet she maintains that our house is "cramped and unsuitable for children". Outside of her, that house has been a foundation and roof over five childrens' heads and stands as twice the size of the bungalow Eleanor resides in. Still, she banters with her tousled hair-do that well, in blatant disregard for her position as advocate...I must somehow take the heat for her obvious transference issues. I don't know. Maybe I remind her of a mother whom she despises...a sister that reigned in all the attention she never received as a child...or possibly a friend that put a finger on the manipulation and deceitfulness of one such Eleanor; post-BFF.

Character Completion

I met Emily on a black Friday. Her last name 'Chesterfield', she was the sole heiress to Chesterfield Arms, her father's pride and joy though Emily was assured she would see not a dime since resuming her mother's lineage via last name. This whole scenario came about as Daddy dearest held taught to greed over the responsibility of a father. No worry though, she was old enough to begin discerning truth for herself and made that bold move in a poignant effort to have Daddy realize what he was missing.

He didn't.

Emily, or 'Em' as we called her, had a way of stopping time long enough to have you consider your stance on an issue and defend it until you made her believe what you now questioned. I am pretty certain she got that trait from her mother, one of my dearest friends, but up to that Friday, had not quite mastered implementing it as casual conversation.

Being a Chesterfield gave her prominence in arms dealing that her mother discovered, really meant nothing if even the signing of such a name was vacant. There was no substance - part of the reason why Em only wrote her name in erasable pen throughout her high school years. This way, she could erase it and script in P-A-R-I-S after showing her father that she'd completed her work. Paris had significance, it had a robustness and a commanding presence. It rolled off the tongue with delightful pronunciation and depending on how much of a pause she put between Em and Paris, which she kept deliberately quip, Em could rattle off her presence 'EmParis' while the corners of her mouth raised in satisfaction with how clever she was becoming in her dawning womanhood.

Gemma on the other hand, Em's mother, had long commanded her own being and gave only as much of herself that she deemed essential for the introduction to continue. If she didn't like you - you were well aware and could somehow deduct that to continue speaking would be an ill investment, not to mention a risk. She meant well. Gemma was strong, intelligent, and had experienced enough vacuous relationships to glean significance from a meeting within a first encounter; a trick that served her well. She appropriately handed down some vice to her daughter and kept enough in her back pocket for when she would inevitably need it.

Shameful

Shameful that your personal growth was stymied long before you reached adulthood. Consequently you have remained in a position of virtual childhood, owing only to immature antics. Shameful that you think even with your entrance upon more than three decades of life, you are somewhat entitled to speak as condescending; act as ego-maniacal as you sound, and most-disappointingly - use our child as your scapegoating pawn in order to get to me.

Do your worst I say. But do your worst to me. Leave out the innocent that you could once identify with. I thought that it was known. You do not manipulate your child. You do not elevate your own agenda by damaging your son. You were unfortunately showered with these same sad and sick behaviors through your quote un-quote youth. You learned first-hand how to hurt, despite allegiance to family. I seriously question at times, whether allegiance of any kind has a place in your life. It certainly does not in relationships, nor in fatherhood. I can speak to its absence in marriage and now our child can attest to its awakening in his own life, led by none other than his own father.

The damaging and hurtful dialogue to your child - by both you and your newly espoused, will affect his psyche for years. It already is. He exchanges doubt with the care that he feels for you and that you squander on a target toward martyring yourself and bringing pain to me. Yet, you are not bringing pain to me except that through our child. He is the one that suffers and questions if you are anything other than empty and mean. I listen intently and give hugs whenever I can. I answer what voids I can account for yet many remain as just that — a void. And mostly, I pray for you. Stymied. That is what you inhabit. A stale, non-expressive existence that must lead you to believe you were forgotten. Your own emptiness is quartered and delivered to those closest to you so that they might do your bidding which you are too cowardice to complete.

I answered tonight with a reply that would make you blush, had you a conscience. He asked me why you hate me so ...why do you hate where I came from with such disdain? I answered: because there...there, he (as in you) had to be a man ...and he could not. There - he had to be accountable, and he failed. And there - he had to be responsible and he did not know how. Here - where he is now requires none of that. It is easy for him (you again) to be spiteful, vengeful and manipulative. It is effortless to be irresponsible, unaccountable and fueled by your self-serving agenda toward defeat.

And what was the worst part?

After all that...after the listening and the explaining...our child gave a half-cocked smirk, closed his eyes and said: "I'm sorry Mommy".

As if he has anything to be blamed for. Yet my pride in seeing a child of a mere eight-years-old taking more responsibility and insight than the man that so candidly hands out psychological warfare — it made me happy and sad. He is going to be far greater, far bigger a man than your greatest desires for a meager existence. There will come a day when you wish you could measure up to the boy that you portrayed as being led astray. And you will not. Your poor presentation as a caring, doting father, will be massively over-shadowed by the child that you irreverently dismissed.

And at that point, that half-smirked grin of his will grow in accordance with my own. I will be the one to apologize for your lacking, shameful solitude, with a hug and an: "I'm sorry son".

To the Attention of Ms. Eleanor Rootes

Ms. Rootes,

This is your client. His name is Garrett. The recent photo is from August, 2011 though you may not recognize this little lad since it has been several months since you have visited him at his father's house. The last recount of you having visited Garrett in my home was ...well, you never have. Pictured next to this dear boy is me, his mother and the one which you proclaim in a closed-door conference amongst attorneys, that you believe to be "too pretty that (she) thinks she can do whatever she wants". A most-unprofessional accusation to make, I would have thought you to be of higher moral character than taking cheap and immature shots which can be interpreted (and rightly so) as partisan and subjective. Though for some time I have thought you to be a impish person with a large, albeit nonsensical opinion for the disdain of me without due cause - I am again saddened to "need" (use of the word need is being weaned from this situation) your loud and obnoxious position within our situation. Why?

Because once again Garrett has climbed into my vehicle at the end of a ridiculous visitation with Dad, with tears in his eyes. Stifling back his innate reaction to cry, he relays that he has had his things taken from him by Dad and told that they would either be "given to a poor family or burned". Most likely, they have already been destroyed. In addition to this, he holds his chest in the spot where he was punched by Dad after being told not to cry, less he gets "something to cry about". There was little to no warning in that situation from the referenced "Dad". Beyond the chest pounding and the illegal seizure of my son's things (Please reference Order on Motion, dated April 9, 2009, page 4, which reads: "ORDERED that Garrett shall be permitted by both parents to bring his belongings back and forth between households and shall be encouraged to bring items upon his expressing a desire to do so". This allowance would be found directly above the notice to

Dad to "not, under any circumstances, ride a motorcycle on a public highway with Garrett on the motorcycle or permit anyone else to do so while Garrett is in his care...". The only reason I again refer to the motorcycle incident is due to the in his care clause. Sadly, Dad is unable, incapable, or completely unwilling to provide care for his son. I have witnessed this time and again. You, if you were any kind of decent, capable, and adept law guardian would too. For whatever the reason, you appear to be enamored with Dad and therefore, disregard and blatantly ill-advise (i.e. LIE) to the court of law which you are bound to uphold the mission of. This does not surprise me either because for six years and counting, you have failed your client to such a fault that he can verbalize your alliance to Dad with clarity.

I have attempted to call you tonight and held my breath while doing so. You live not two miles from my own home and yet, have never stopped. I stopped counting the number of phone calls placed over six years when I got to 77. I stopped thinking about how sickening your acting position is when you attempted to weasel your way into a situation which you knew/know nothing of outside of Dad's rantings. And yet still, after watching my child relay what could be into the triple digits of a story count for tales befallen him by his Dad, I called you. Because YOUR JOB is to act as the voice for children that do not contain the vocabulary or comprehension of the unfortunate domestic situation(s) that their parents are in. Because you have taken (supposedly) an oath to Do No Harm to those same children and to speak with ease and comfort, to hear their limited vocabularies describe situations that a decent parent never wishes upon their child - and to then take that sullen story to a Judge who will make a conscious and clear-headed decision for the well-being of the child.

Yet, you fail. You have failed my child many times over and you continue still. You seek the admiration of a crowd you are not fit to stand before. Your lame attempts at vengeance and ill will toward me come as nothing other than a transference of hatred you must hold toward someone else. I can take it. Raised with accountability and responsibility; I can take it. My child; your client should not have to.

Your phone beeped without connection. You must not have power on the other side of the hill - so I stood there thinking of a way that I could get out the information that you absolutely need to heed. Which brings me to the present: Life does not operate on a nine to five schedule. Most situations which you are charged to recount for the sake of any court of law occur either before or after such luxuries. I do not expect you to suddenly decide to do the right thing because at half a decade's worth of time, you have neglected to do the right thing. What I do expect is for you to see that you are harming those same persons - children - because of your obstinate comprehension of your duty and to therefore, remove yourself. For a child of eight years old to accurately recount the whereabouts of your timely visits with his Dad...for him to be so discouraged at realizing what he told you in confidence, what you swore was between you and he - to watch you march directly to Dad and relay only the pertinent details keeping Dad in your favor - it is grotesque. You are not there when the reactions hit. You are not there when he is pummeled for crying, hit for speaking, or mocked for knowing. And the most repulsive part? You do not seem to care. So please, do my son as well as any other child entrusted to your position as Law Guardian a huge favor: RESIGN.

You know my number,

Patricia

Mediocre Minds

Great spirits have always encountered violent opposition from mediocre minds.

- Albert Einstein

Burden

Burden comes in such depths of weight. Today, as if all other days were semi-significant - was elemental in change. A step toward difference. A leap toward manifestation. I sat patiently awaiting my turn; scraping random food parts from my pants and tapping the toes of my boots to a wall-to-wall carpet that begged for a vacuum.

"Trish, you can go in now," came a voice from behind the half-wall of justice. I stood, and ran my hands over my pleats, wrestled all handles into a convenient grouping and threw shoulders back before walking. My mother always told me to stand up straight - that point resonated on this day. The solemn march to a back office where I might find a plush, leather chair and an all-to-anxious legal representative, salivating over my arrival.

"Have a seat".

Thank you, I'll stand...I used the next three and a half minutes to lay out before him, my myriad of jargon and attempted justification.

"The problem...is that you're giving me numbers that don't match. There must be something that I am missing. What am I missing Trish?"

"Mmmm - well, how much time do you have?"(On the inside).

On the outside, I drew attention to the process that has aided and abetted such a criminal - the thundering march of drums growing louder within - "there is a process," I chant.

Elements of change came in the form of understanding. I detailed and derailed, drifted and scaffolded what would otherwise be a migraine-at-will. And finally, the look of ah. ha. came to the surface. I think he gets it. My point, my reasons, my challenge toward being a better human.

I cried this morning as I cry at night. No more a bleeding-heart than the next occupied citizen, I want out of this sickness. In the slap of a pen to yellow legal pad and a smirk which signified comprehension, I was suddenly lighter. In as many years and equal sleepless nights, I have worried. If only....

There is no answer yet, but I remain vigilant. In so much as I can understand the elements that cause growth, change, ...becoming, I can understand this. Oh, to be something other than the targeted. It is happening though. An evolution. Still, I stand. I teeter to the right - sway back to the left - there is balance here in this movement. I miss them. I miss being looked upon as if I had all the answers. I am good at this even though you question my motivations. I am good at taking care - at care-taking. I am meant for this - justifier to the unjust; advocate for the forgotten.

Remind me when those drums chant louder. Recall the pounding reinforcements of sacrifice and the deafening pounds of vision; of fortitude. They march.

They need care too.

What She Wasn't

There were days that itemizing the lists of things surrounding her existence came as a priority to other actions; possibly breathing. She wasn't rich. She didn't own the best of anything outside her husband and children, and she wasn't sure of where to go when she thought she was lost. She knew that she could pray, but sometimes praying didn't seem enough. She prayed anyway.

She didn't own much of anything that was new, and she deliberately shopped for things that were not new. She believed that "new" meant little more than "more cheaply made". She kept breathing when it got too hard to draw a deep breath and she kept thinking when her brain did little more than hum like a static-filled radio station. Think, think, think. She hasn't had time to herself in more than half a decade and even that's okay. She would gladly give away all that she owns for the smile it might bring to someone else, or the warmth, or the comfort, the understanding, the enjoyment, the belief.

She fiddled with her new ring; spinning it 'round and 'round her finger until it stopped like a spun bottle on the clock striking twelve - the glass slipper left on the front step, the disbelief, the confusion...what happened? Where did she go?

She was on a mission. One that was known only to her and those select few that shared her thoughts, her whispers and who actually listened. She had calculated and planned and yet, there was so very much room left that did not make sense.

She prayed again. Spinning the ring again, spinning the thoughts. It had to lead to some form of materialized event. There had to be a reason. Where the hell did the slipper go?! What was "she" - as all that embodies "she" missing? Where did she go wrong? What was so big, or small, or huge, or insignificant - that she missed it? Mission. Reckless endangerment of self - she had belief. She knew that. She had faith. She fully and wholeheartedly understood that.

With one shoe on and one off, she marched on with a smile.

Her eyes spoke louder than the smile on her face, but she marched. Consequences be had, she marched.

Truth Has its Pardons

Here I sit at 11:11 in the p.m. recollecting the day's events. I have glorious friends who fill my life to the brim, children whom I am proud, yet stern with, and a love that makes an endless smile spread across my face. Thinking so fondly of those whom I love brought me to the sequester of the online world in late hours, the time where one sits and somewhat mindlessly stumbles through the pages of the communication age. I signed in just as I should to my photo portal, and entered under the search bar for "soul mate". Just that - two words that are entirely meaningful and would certainly pull up symbolic photos which I could promptly copy and paste to my love's page. A momentary reminder that I think of him now, thought of him just a second ago, and will think of him in just another moment. Soul mate.

I get the hour glass and take a spot of wine. Hmmmm.....

"No searches match your query".

Lame.

Dumb.

We are the communication age! We have all facilities at our fingertips to think, inspire, create, regress, and transpire into something, all things...great...and nothing matches soul mate?! I am utterly irritated. Just for a moment though. Because after just a thought or two I realize that communication or not, creativity and then some, and with a splash of technology in this little ranch house - the point remains that the feelings, the inspiration for life still (Only) exists in life. Soul mates do exist and I bet my last and only two dollars on that fact. There is a reason for our plodding. A masterful technological piece of machinery is, itself skeptical and intolerant of those situations it cannot replicate: i.e. soul mates.

Take back seat technology and communication outside my speech. I laugh at your insignificance yet depend upon it (to an extent), I take note of your indecision and am enthralled at the hierarchy of love yet again.

Praise, praise. Thinking more highly of our accomplishment, I offer you a toast Lovey — even high tech industrial science doesn't know what to do with a love like ours!

Shed

A bow is drawn slowly; elegantly across the strings of an instrument singly sweetly to emotion: it bleeds. It is a weeping, sorrowful song that enlightens. One long elicited note that sings to reconciliation and suddenly, there is a sense of clarity. In the distant, there is a strumming - a smooth beat which summons strength. What is brewing?

Ability.

And where from here?

...only God knows.

The Shovel Theory

Here's how it works:

Take any person and hand them a shovel. It doesn't have to be expensive, or fiberglass, or colorful ... just a shovel. What would they do? Personally, I have no less than six ideas right off the top of my head that I could, would, should institute a shovel into in order that they work. The man (and/or woman) with a quote-unquote blue collar would know exactly how to incorporate a shovel if handed one. And the suggestion of getting it for free? Bonus.

But to the politician, the professional talker or the famed representative that thrives on nepotism and one hand washing the other - my guess is that they would be rendered speechless. That, or they would think me a lunatic. For several years I have disclosed one such shovel theory to my friends and family on the occasion that we have a few moments to chat and eat and laugh. And tonight, that shovel theory reached a whole new level. Now, the shovel theory lends its well-conceived intellect to what we're calling the "Get to Work" campaign for government officials.

I propose that we collect shovels. One by one, those shovels are mailed to each state/district representative with an enclosed motivational speech to read: "Get to Work". The follow-up campaign to this is documentary photographs of real, honest and hard-working individuals who show their hands in a picture with a nicely fonted sub-statement to read: "I have calluses, do you?". See to the working person, the shovel is useful. It is an assist, a tool, a means to an end...it is necessary. Yes, to some it may be little more than a prop, but still - I would bet they have calluses to show they can use a shovel to produce something. But to the persons elected to positions of power that do the talking for all their constituents, a shovel is nearly useless. Heck, if it was a pen they would be more obliged to motivate. An embossed pen and the promise of your vote, and they'll send a postage paid Christmas card. Excuse me, holiday card.

So what to do? I'm thinking that I shall begin tomorrow anew by collecting those pennies that I subconsciously pick up on the sides of sidewalks and store fronts and beneath store shelves - and I'm going to save. Save until I have enough to buy the first of what will become many, shovels. Sent straight away to the congressman or woman of my district with that enclosed notation: "Get to Work". I will most-definitely include a picture of my hands since they do have many the callous, and I'll begin documenting the responses. Donations will be gratefully accepted and we might even get so far as to embossing handles and creating memorabilia in honor of those hard working individuals and families who know all-too-well what it means to work with their hands day in and day out without the expectation of gratitude. And if Washington doesn't like my shovels. I'll give them to those that will truly appreciate it.

PS: I do have a PayPal account.

Gratefully,

Shovel Theory

The Hitch

Bullies don't ever stop being bullies. Much like leopards - their spots remain the same. There is a movement against the antics of bullies and those that support such foolishness. The greater good is that bullies are not welcome in most social spheres. The hitch is that in this case, the bully is dad. An individual who laughs at a little boy's tears and is maddened by any support in spite of his own freakish behavior. I seek for another name or title, but most of what I conjure is depreciating and (though valid) doesn't encompass the full range of destitute that belongs to this ... thing. Let's back up a bit, shall we?

7pm: we're waiting in the driveway.

7:10pm: through a dim driveway light comes the sullen figure of a little boy, dragging behind him his belongings with drooping shoulders.

7:12 - 7:20pm: come the story of how said thing taunted and teased, punched, smacked and kicked him while he attempted to gather his things because his mom (me) was waiting outside. The bullying went on for fifteen minutes, maybe twenty...where thing and thing's cousin made fun of my little boy. He mentioned that as he raised his hands to his face in order to deflect a blow from dad, dad's cousin kicked him in the side. And as he fell to the floor and asked no less than five times to "please stop" - Dad and cousin told him that he would be caught in many a fight because he's "a pussy"...that he should tear off the ear of his opponent and show it to him/her and that they would then go into shock, rendering him the winner....that he needs to "learn how to fight" (said through slurred and staggered speech as supported by the empties around the house)...that he probably had his card turned in school (a behavioral modification in the classroom) because you were looking at other boys' *expletive* (parts)... and that he wasn't to "bullshit (his) mother when you tell her this story".

7:21pm: Gasping cries evidenced this little boy's hopelessness as he proclaimed: "He says he loves me but he acts like he doesn't. I don't like him. I'm not going back".

7:22pm: "I'm not going back there".

7:23pm: "I'm not going back".

7:25pm: "Mom, please don't make me go back there".

7:27 - 9:58pm: Now finally asleep in his bed, my mind continues to stir with heavy emotions and bitter, bitter anger. Bound by words on paper that entail every detail of life, I feel I am rendered as helpless as I know my child feels. In good conscience I cannot take him there — allow him to be entrusted to the "care" of a thing that is no better than an immature imbecile who revels in loathsome antics that serve only to belittle, disparage and depreciate others. If he can get in a tormenting punch, or slap, hit, kick, shove, or festering tease - he does.

And yet, I - as a mother, am supposed to be an accomplice to the delivery of my child to a person that should not have anything to do with, or around children. Bullies = abusive parasites / parasites = bullies. Have to remove the feeding grounds.

Skeletons & Seeds

"Geronimo!" she yelled as she put two argyle sock-covered feet into pant legs that were not flared enough at the bottoms. She was beginning to like herself on the outside and love herself on the inside though she still battled those demons of self-doubt and questioning. She was always questioning…if she had done the right thing, enough of the right thing…if she could do more. Just the evening before now, she had been inspired to paint – and pulling a cigar box of water-colored pigment from beneath her plants, dropped a picture of that little boy who breathed life into her world. She'd picked it up and ran her hand across the heart-shaped framed face of her then six-year-old, pictured in his red tie and black fedora. Had three years gone by so quickly that it felt as if it were yesterday? Yes, they had.

She knew he was learning, growing and experiencing everything – understanding only a fraction of it, similarly to her own situation. What concerned her most were the effects that many, many, too many to count situations of abuse, neglect…of psychological warfare upon her child, were having. Intrinsically, she understood that the Mom title afforded her the "best preventative medicine" award, but time moved so quickly. Too quickly. It was like that skeleton and seed analogy she'd drawn the other day; the similarity between the strength of a skeleton and potential of a seed.

She had walked past the wind-blown and weather-worn remnants of a lily seed pod for months. There were no flowers remaining, no foliage, and no green - just the skeletal remnants of a pod which had, at one point, held the seeds for another year of beauty promised by that unseen potential. Had she been there in that garden in September, she may have cut them back when the flowers faded, thinking that besides helping the plant to rejuvenate roots before autumn, nobody enjoys looking at the stalky reminders of a summer almost gone. But she wasn't there in September, or even October. On the first day of February, she found those skeletal memories and recalled the passing of another year. The pods had transpired the wind, all elements of accumulation and even a quick judgment by the would-be gardener, had she been present. They were beautiful, those masterpieces of transparent mirrors between what was and what might be. She picked them and put them in a vase to admire. To remind myself. What had her perspective overlooked or neglected when she was certain she was seeing the whole picture?

Mostly, it is the difficulty with the space-time continuum. As in – there does not seem to be enough space to ignore what happens to her little boy all the time. Reflections. She reminisced on those lilies again. They were thought to be dead, used up, done – and yet, she picked them because they were perfect. Like her little boy – no matter the wicked elements put-upon him, he was still perfect; beautiful. He was worth preserving with her greatest concoction of preventative medicine. And at this point as a weary traveler, it may come down to a huge "Geronimo" of faith.

After the Facts

Fact 1: My son is continuously abused by his father

Fact 2: The courts, to this point have been unable to properly attend to the needs of this situation or assign accountability in order to keep my son safe.

Fact 3: My son is honest; yet frustrated, hurt; but maintaining, strong; and growing all the wiser by the day.

Fact 4: The litany of charges against said father (see also "Pop", "Abuser"), psychological turmoil and abuse at the hands of said father, and undeniable harm is a real and present danger for my son Every. Week.

Fact 5: "The Hitch" (see below) happened only a week ago. This means that juggling the emotions, the hurt, the upset and anger is something that will take time to contend with.

Fact 6: Abusers are enabled by those closest to them (e.g. family, friends) who fail to, or cannot see the truth

Fact 7: My responsibility and role as mother means that I must, at all times, protect the physical, social, emotional, and psychological well-being of my child to the absolute best of my ability.

Given the facts – the unfettered allowance for the transgressor to continue violating the rights of others means a little boy is berated, conditioned and abused continuously. Please refer to those facts as I explain the following:

Abuser fights for every-other weekend visitation because he play-acts as if he cares about the time spent with his son. Abusers are granted weekend visitation, plus Monday and Tuesday evenings for a few hours. Law-guardian (a.k.a. : Abuser's second attorney of record) supports this arrangement as it was she who rallied for Pop / Abuser to have more time in support of her "that Mom is alienating" claim - unsupported as it was. I could carry on volumes about the law-guardian's moral reprehension, but I'll leave that for another day. This is about the abuser emboldened by a failed system. So, my son returns from a weekend visitation having spent little to no time with the person having claimed he needed more time, and Monday's "long talk with Pop that I didn't like" bore statements akin to brainwashing. As proof, I present (and paraphrase):

"Because you're honest and tell your Mom what's happening here, you are making (my second wife leave)…she's leaving me and it's yours and your mother's fault." "…I cannot continue being a father to someone who makes up stories just to hurt me, or get me in trouble" "Your Mom records everything that you say so she can get me into trouble because she just wants to take you away…You are misunderstanding what I did to you…you hit me as much as I hit you, right? I wasn't drinking when I did that to you…when I and my (twenty-something) cousin mocked you and punched you, I didn't kick you or laugh at you…we didn't do more of the same actions when you asked us five times to 'please stop'…you imagined it and you helped do it too…you hurt me too, didn't you?…are you sorry now?…do you see why you can't tell your Mother what happens here?…if you keep telling her and other people, than I can't be your father, you understand?".

This amounts to a sobbing and depreciated little boy questioning, at the end of the night, what he did so wrong that the man who fathered him, not only blames him but "doesn't love me, Mom".

After-the-facts torture and abusers will always abuse.

Fact 7: My responsibility and role as mother means that I must, at all times, protect the physical, social, emotional, and psychological well-being of my child to the absolute best of my ability.

Barely, if at all.

I have barely acknowledged the velocity and impact of a life unexamined, or in the right perspective - acknowledged the continuance of hurt from those elements of a life unexposed. I want to write, to paint those stories of news for experiences which have led me to this place. I am afraid. I want to expose those tyrants that draw blood and do not stop - though it seems for all my efforts, they continue without pause, and (particularly) without remorse or countenance. Their faces are hidden in ways that escape me. I see them for who they are but to outside persons, they are as normal as the definition. All that said, I write in metaphors and operate in hallucinations. Why? It is painful. It's brutal. The struggle day in and day out with what I have been left. I care not for the material, but rather for the emotive context of things. And that is exactly what was bruised and battered.

Although I sound like I'm whining, I'm not. I'm simply pissed. ...and baffled. And aggravated at this exchange. If you could see him. See the way that he operates in daylight versus the behavior that happens when I show up on-scene. And how does one get that part into the light? It is not for lack of trying, I assure you. A year ago I wrote a resolution that led to the impending New Year. I swore I would be more forgiving, more outright, more...forgiving. And in honesty, I have. Yet he does not forgive me. I am tired of struggling with my thoughts and emotions with no return but a beat-down via those powers-that-be. Those same powers that promise to uphold the law and "protect and serve". What a joke. Truth is, I want a return. I want an apology, and a listening ear as invested in my speech as I am when I promise to listen. I want someone, something to make this right and so far, it just drags...on, and on...and on...and on...and on.

On some days when the sun is high in the sky and I listen intently to the silence, I am fine. I can understand and progress on blind faith. Most days are like that really. Blind faith.

Cessation

Downside: My face is breaking out as if I've just hit puberty. I grab the extra-strength cleanser received from my dearest esthetician friend and slather my pores to shut them up. Morning rolls around and I realize I fell asleep in my day clothes again with my knitted scarf choking the stale air out of me as it is still wrapped around my neck. The cleanser has managed to create pools of sloughing skin on my chin, right cheek and left temple. Joy.

I make a mental note to reorganize the bedroom later and put those pillow cases in the laundry. Turns out that fleece bedding, though warm, wicks away all moisture and does nothing for your complexion. Those pesky sun spots are off-setting the dry skin patches now that I look closely at my reflection in the iridescent lighting of a cold, tin building.

How did I end up here?

If I had a belted jacket and some padding to slam myself against, I might feel more secure with this placement. And for as much as I know I shouldn't say that, my hurdles of stalled motivation are growing larger by the day. So far this morning, I have adjusted the thermostat four times and tried to rework the dirty looks I am inspired to give to the guard who is never lacking a sarcastic retort. I recount the times that my heart has smiled in this most recent past and I realize that it hovers there; my heart. It stays in a place of comfort, afraid to push out into the cold because we are not quite ready to step ahead. There's no boo-hooing, just adrift. My daily conversations with God tell me to wait – that I have put it out there and now I must just wait. Physical symptom number one which occurs when I become impatient and stressed…my eyes twitch - that's happening. Just behind my left eye socket an irritating little finger scratches at my temporal lobe reminding me that I am not quite where I want to be and can do nothing about it at the present moment.

Buggers.

Brick by Brick

A solar flare at 5am burst rays of light through dusty drapes and shone like spotlights on the many home projects not yet completed. "Yeah, yeah" I murmur as I turn the other way and flop down on my feather pillow just in time to have the alarm blare in my face and blink 5-2-2…5-2-2…5-2-2 a.m. until I fist pound the snooze button on top.

My definition of friend has changed, as has how I define commitment, achievement, passion…depression. It could be that Cinnamon, the nurse practitioner was right when she told me that I didn't "look depressed" five years ago. Curious if she would change her opinion today? Of course, does it matter when the greater challenge is taking someone named "Cinnamon" seriously?

I am five months into the greatest defining moment of my life today and yet it's that solar flare highlighting my stagnated home projects that controls my thoughts. To be honest, those thoughts also compete with a failed political system, rising gas prices, the search for employment and neglectful parents. I go to work each day thankful for the consistent schedule yet yearning for the impassioned mind of being home and being free.

A friend spoke just today of this wrestling jive. The "rebuild to fall" of everyday situations we plan and ponder, create, step back, admire and then *crash*. The Jenga brick supporting most of the weight gets pulled too quickly and the tower falls down. In that respect, we are somewhat of a thick-headed …no, persevering population huffing and puffing in our tumbled messes and then reorganizing until we have

another base on which to build. Brick by brick the plan is reconstructed with adjustments made where we guess our weak points were the first time.

The supports of strength come through in our rebuilding with the relationships we cultivate; prioritizing those closest to us first and fashioning our thoughts of hope and faith with functionality and some linear logic – at least enough to get those mental blueprints stamped approved. As it was, I am a particularly mutable substance transformed with all things musing and dissolving into a useful element of empathy. How depleting this can be. I am committed however. So my choice is really not a choice, but an assured response to do what is right, necessary and expected of that mutability.

Rebuilding ...

Evidently

1995 was the year of the penny picked up and measured in due profit to her cause.

Of late, she militated, wanting to say something valuable but stifled it for the solution of vagueness she knew it marinated in. With a deep breath in pulled down past her diaphragm and into the belly, she mustered the courage to back up all statements with faith that all would be well in the end, everything would work out as it was supposed to and the push and pull of what to do and when was the exactness of free choice and humanity.

The surging pulse grew from the inside. It beat like a bass drum from a far-off hillside but grew closer every time she feigned her preparedness to speak. She had a buffet of thoughts and subjects to choose from, yet it was never enough of that one thing to expedite the voice. A

dull "well" would usually surface, followed by the ever-anticipatory "Nothing"…still, no golden-globe.

What kept her silent?! Heads up, tails up it didn't matter. Friend or foe, she would listen and friend or foe she would empathize. Yet, there was still nothing to be said about the greater challenge she was facing. Mornings were similar to evenings…similar to afternoons and the same as the in-between times. Silent. Nothing to say. The swell of energy for verbiage would often result in tears and they ran back down the face; materializing as the unspoken words she sought.

What goes up…

Evidently, she was not supposed to speak right now. Proven perspective: when one sense is not 100% the other senses magnify to make up for the loss. Logistically then, not speaking actualizes listening.

Turns out what is more difficult than speaking what she is not exactly certain she should speak of?…listening without speaking. Tasked.

The Recipe

Blue and clear glass canning jars with the lids reused, were washed and placed bottoms-side up in the dish drainer in preparation. Yes, there was enough room on the shelf high above the food products and deliberately out of reach. The red step ladder was placed beneath and the curtain pulled back to disclose the space that would soon be closed up for good.

Bitterness went in the first jar with the lid fastened tightly and the jar pushed all the way to the left. Jealousy was next and the contents were siphoned down as the jar was tapped repeatedly on the counter to get the product to settle. Anger, resentment and jaded went into wide-mouth containers. It seemed she had a bulk of those, though spite, malice, fury, cynicism, and annoyance ran a close second. Every pain and poison was poured and ladled into their new glass houses. Some blue, some clear — they each had a home and would hereby be measured by volume, not by weight as they were far too heavy to carry any longer.

Hatred, in its abundance, took up the space of three jars — the biggest ones. Four quarts each made a full dozen in quarts of poison. Shameful. What was left after that, she swept from the floor and wiped from the counters into a dust pan. This was promptly emptied into the toilet and flushed. Twice. Regret, envy and worry were the last to go and were layered like a sand sculpture, revealing swirling folds of red-hued pain now encased in the tallest of glass testimonials. She guessed that this might cure her affliction with heartburn, hereafter.

And then — like a cookie crumble-crusted and cream-filled hot pocket of goodness, she started again. Faith was the bottom layer and a requirement for this home-maker guru. Courage, adventure, and determination were mixed to a fulfilling base. Spunk, bravery and valor would be blended with spirit to develop a savory crust but would be set aside for the moment. Flavors and energy had to marry while she folded mojo, moxie and grit in on themselves to balance such a rich concoction. These were her most favorite ingredients — splashes of moxie and drizzles of mojo.

The nourishment was sure to be satisfying, yet leave her hungry for more. It was designed this way as an ideal fuel source. The taste would be inspiring; the delivery impeccable. She gave thanks in advance for what she already knew would be bestowed upon her. Joy, peace, contentment and calm were whipped to a stiff peak and refrigerated only until she could pour on the mojo, moxie, and grit sauce, which had become exquisitely aromatic. Lastly, she grated a fine coating of trust over the top and set down her tools.

A step back. Idyllic temptation.

While it baked to a convection perfection she would draw closed that curtain on the top shelf and wipe down the counters. And salivating in anticipation, something about her just knew that this was the answer all along.

The Road

I remember the day you were sick and would only calm your crying when I would rock-a-bye you in the blue chair that now sits on my front porch. You were four when I left and hard as it was to go, it was something I needed to do. More than a decade later and my actions are driving to get my family home. Funny in a way – how I left, collected my own little family and now want to show them what I had (have) as a wonderful life.

So why did that late night conversation wear on us so? I think it's because we wish for time that has passed too quickly while we might have been asleep and desire to change the circumstances that leave us wondering now. And you – you're more awake that I was at your age. In the words of John Lennon, "you may say that I'm a dreamer…" Yes, I am. A blessing and a block, dreaming is. For me, dreaming is a coping mechanism (for escape) and a planning tool for reality…for manifesting.

And for us – this whole journey, both my independent journey and yours…have been intertwined and crossed many times o'er. They're supposed to be. In a way, they have been reflections for the other person. Kind of like me running a test, failing, and relaying back to you not to do that same thing. In that case, I've been like a researcher. In the meantime, you encourage, inspire and assist with so very much of my life that I'm forever indebted to that huge heart of yours. And

both of us walk, talk and speak the line. We try to anyway and that is the point. To continue doing what is right, what is best and what should be done, regardless of the circumstances we find ourselves in. I know that I get stuck somewhere between want and need at times. When I think that things should just be easier, be clearer…be over, and they aren't, that is the real test of faith. For the moments in time when things could have gone differently we have to recognize them as insights for that moment. We are here. And here, we are together.

The Right to Write: Monarks

I am mostly raw. Bare bones adjusting turns to keep Spring winds from gusting through my rib cage and bringing about too many gasps from the floating head on top of a spinal column with slight curvature. Yesterday's ravens made carrier pigeons look as bedazzled as a peacock – as they laughed mockingly at my forward (slowed, but still forward) movement to make things righted again.

At 12:23pm I received a phone call from the school…something, something full body rash…something, "yes, pick him up." Engage instinct. In less than an hour I arrived at a monitor affixed to a brick wall and adjusted my dress in the mirrored doors. I pushed the big, black button, wishing it were red and then answered the static-ridden "*garble, garble can I help you?*" from the wall box.

"Yes, I'm here for my son". The doors unlock.

And as quickly as I am inside, the desire to get back out again jumps to the front of the line. I go through the motions though: sign the pink sheet, initial, date, half-smile, palm breath-check, quasi-admire art work that's outdated, sigh on the inside, decide which one of the three clocks in the room I want to reference for the time (they're each different) …and wait.

The waiting part gets the most response. Similar to visiting a zoo to find the lioness on the outside of the bars – you're gawked at. It is the perfect opportunity for onlooker to throw supposition and what-if theories into the wind and see whose gossipy ad-libs are most favored. Like, "maybe they let her out on purpose?". I could have saved the Monarks time by proclaiming them all winners and chewing on my arm or sucking on the end of my sweater sleeve. That seems too easy though. I'm not sure what my latest ailment by their count is anymore. I would have to throw the wow-factor in there if I wanted to trip them up.

I started thinking *maybe unkempt and woodsy…or becoming a deliberate fashion faux-pas…possibly painted and rail thin, make them think I'm depressed and medicated*. I stopped when I realized I had just described **78%** of the population or thereabouts. Turns out that acting normal and keeping it together is more of a host for presumption than drooling on yourself or eating random paint chips. I had thought myself amusing for wearing dangly earrings that clanged against my necklace like wind chimes; certainly, straightening my hemline before being seen publicly would make them wonder. Eh, anyway.

I queried the artwork for origination, read something about a "community of learners" and counted floor tiles on my way to the classroom. I waited again. And then two, three, four ladies came out, gave me the once-over and then returned to their learning den. Lioness. Outside. Bars. No words uttered, but I filled in the script with what I knew was being thought: "Oh, yyyoou're his Mommmm, ohhhh…". I almost wanted to do the thought-process aloud for them: "Now you take what you see and add it to what you thought you knew about me. Just like legos! See how they don't match? Yea, that means that one piece doesn't fit with the other one. I'm sorry, but you're going to have to make sure you have the right information to go with the correct observation, okay? Ohhkay."

big smile, lots of teeth.

Not long after I had my son in-tote and we skipped out the front doors, saying goodbye to the wall box until our next showing.

This Ain't Nothing

Friday's mental siphoning usually happens on the drive to and from work. Considering options, the weighing of alternative routes, and roads less traveled – it generally shows up in blips and blurbs of thought. Today being a Friday, the course continued as I ticked away the minutes following 18-wheeled flatbeds and milk haulers up the Thruway. I give friendly waves to the milk haulers. I figure we need them to know they're important and are of the few and proud left helping to feed this country.

My mp3 player buzzes on with the song Every Reason Not to Go and I am reminded of my dear baby sister playing that same song and singing along as a reminder to my brother. At the time, he was dreaming of the consideration to work at crop harvesting and the very idea of him leaving left all of us excited, yet sad. He stayed; for now. But I could hear her singing as I listened and put my blinker on to move into the right-hand lane for someone who appeared to have a much more important place to go than I.

Thoughts: *every reason not to go…how about every reason TO go? How about that? Let's see, number four-hundred and seventy three would be:

— No matter the direction you point from our house at the center of Main Street, you would find friends, family, love

— Where we work hard with the feeling of sweat on our shirts

Monday through Friday, and even Saturdays – but we pray for the chance to do it again the next week

- Where Sunday morning church service is a reminder to do better, to do right and to do the best that you possibly can every day

- Where street signs stand as memory markers for years of reminiscing on what it means to be raised well

- Where greenery flourishes: happy plants equal happy heart

- Where there's good food on the table and music in the air

- The stars! January through December they're outstanding, all wrapped in a blanket of Milky Way and falling periodically through the night sky with just the right amount of time to place a wish

- Where accountability marries responsibility – that's a good one

- Community – have we forgotten? Family, friends, neighbors working to support encourage and understand each other – that makes a community

- Where I will write my books, paint my art, raise my family, teach and cook and clean and entertain those well off and less fortunate than I which gives us culture.

- And mostly – the reason to go: Family. (They are my heroes, they are my weakness)

All that I could muster at this point, was the desperate plea: "God, please protect us and show me how…". As I spoke, a car pulled in front of me from the right and my shuffled mix of songs switched to the next in line. The crystal hanging from the rear-view mirror dangled like a pendulum and I look ahead to the car that was so hasty in their driving. That's when I noticed the license plate ahead read: "UR VALUE", the song played on with the words "This Ain't Nothin'" and the sun shining through my windshield passed through that pendulum and showered me in rainbows. Promise. Remember the promise.

And there was peace.

The Legacy

At some point in every parent's life, I believe you reach for the idea that you might be so lucky to leave behind a legacy with your life. By example of living well and learning much, you want for your children to replicate your good deeds and recall your greatness. You wish for the difficult times to evaporate into loving memories of how doing right is always harder, but always worth it - how your efforts as a parent made the life you led momentous to the life your children will lead.

When you reach for this legacy, what used to be personal highlights: anniversaries, birthdays, the coming of age, sleep – they lose importance against the needs of your family. Nearly overnight your husband and children are prioritized. You bask in their happiness, their joy and accomplishments, taking little to no credit for what, intrinsically, you know has been in due part to your being their mother. You just smile.

This is how a legacy is born – where the rewards are reaped years beyond the seeds being sown. But aspirations for great heights, for excellence as a human being, for repenting those mistakes made and finding they were grand gestures to completion – they were counted. And eventually, maybe on the eve of some forgotten anniversary or the happening of another birthday – every piece falls into perfect placement ~ your legacy is born.

That is today.

You have done it Mom. You have been the action and reaction to what it means to live on Faith, and act on Love. We, as your children, are indebted because there is no greater accomplishment than what we have been granted as a Mother. There is no reason to ever not try harder and appreciate more, because we have front-row seats to excellence in life.

Thank you Mom.

And Happy Birthday.

Evermore,

Your Children

To Know Her is to Love Her

Are you aware that October 20th is the official holiday of "Sweetest Day"? Yep. I got an email notification this morning indicating as much. The irony in this case is that I just sat with you last evening and I can see you're laden with worry, but you are as silent as you are strong. There are times when the bother is allowed to pass on its own. This, however, is not one of those times.

Something has you tied up; something has you withdrawn. I have my own lists of guesses as to what that might be, but more than guessing I think that you need to be reminded often of what everyone else sees when they look at you. I'm taking a leap here and speaking for most, if not all, of humanity when I say that we see strength. We see ability. We see and experience a beauty of you that is incomparable even the definition of beautiful. We see the most-incredible springing to life of a being that God could make. We see, and most of us know, that the process of becoming can be a slow one. ...One that is not easy, not always happy, and certainly not light - But one which is worth it. Particularly when it is someone as becoming as you are.

You will be taxed with this weight. You will be responsible for an incredible load that seems, at times, too much for someone so young, so trusting and non-judgmental. Quite frankly, you will be responsible for this because God gave you a heart that is entirely too big for your body. It was no mistake – there is a reason even in that. Mostly, because you can carry it and ultimately, because it is the process of blooming. So let that spirit shine on – forgive often, worry less, and let it be. Exist in some acceptance that there is a plan and there is purpose for you. And if nothing else, know that I plan to celebrate Sweetest Day with you, if you'll have me. Times like these are sought after by many. You are at the helm dear one – so shine on!

…and we see love.

For He Who is Her All

She waited with bated expectation for the man who governed her world. He would present just as soon as the silver lining to their already magnificent dream, appeared. They knew it would happen, and on most days she was able to forgo the wart of worry that was slowly metastasizing on her forehead, for the Chardonnay conversationalists she touted to in the evening. They seemed to understand her speech as she recalled the memories of her man and they would nod in agreement as her eyes drifted upward toward the window with query of a new arrival. Fridays were her favorite day because they closed the gap on all of the concern brewed in 1-degree weather throughout the week.

She remedied to remind him at each turn of conscience that he was the very reason for everything in her life. Often, he would smile, get

a warmed expression and remind her of the same. The onslaught of romanticism would grow each time that she saw him and somewhat sicken her Chardonnay guests. It was worth it though.

Never would he be caught, senility or not, without knowing - with absolute certainty, that she loved him and that destiny had befallen their marriage.

Relevance of the Scorekeeper

Initially, the idea was to weigh happenstances against experience and decipher enough of the situation to tell if I had progressed. In theory, the idea was manageable – upon initiation however, it is proving quite difficult. The lines of reference are skewed to allow for only small portions of progress when I really feel like I am walking backwards, instead of forward.

And so, I am contemplating.

Contemplation always seems to help in some manner. Life perspective is a multistep scenario: see it. Process it. Implement it. Allocate the outcome by screening out the trouble. I am, I believe – looped in the processing stage. A lot. What this amounts to is that I keep score against myself rather than for myself; an epiphanial-tragedy. That is what I shall deem this exercise of a thought-provoked existence. Epiphanial-tragedy. I get a great idea and make dire efforts toward initiating or implementing it for myself or family, and then …I falter. So in essence, the score-keeping is the marked effort that is in fact, holding me back.

In essence, our daily processing becomes the start of a new story every day while altering the ending as we go; an endless do-over opportunity. The magic however, is in the act of letting go of the process; the score-keeping and enabling that whole "like begets like" action, to occur by putting out there what we want to get back. My mother would often say that "the more you give, the more you get," which to the ten-year-old, insinuated the physical giving: clothes, belongings, money. The same is true for the metaphysical – love, care, energy – these elements when given, bring more of the same in return. And how does one plagued with the epiphanial-tragedy keep score against that? Instead of a savings account, it is an investment portfolio chock full of high-yield eternal stocks.

It's like country singer Dwight Yoakam emphasized in his song, Waterfall: "my heart still believes that love for what we need, can be enough". It can and is enough – so long as the tally marks don't form alongside the action. And with that, we do have everything.

By Purpose & Passion: Connecting the Dots

If all great changes are preceded by chaos, this is going to be epic.

My well-roundedness can sometimes be lost in translation. This is the thought pattern that occurs as I perch; the glorified receptionist whose brain and exuberance are metastasizing. With each phone call that comes through, I answer with less enthusiasm than the one before it; counting the tick-tick-tock of state issued equipment. I write, I think, I paint, sketch, pray, plan and scheme while working – yet, I am not complete until I go home. "Don't gripe or complain" the voice o'er my left side calls – "you're working while a majority of the population is unemployed".

"But don't forget," comes the right, "that every day you're not doing what you should be, you are losing time that you will never get back". The arguing and logic lines continue like this for some time until one or the other gives in to economic reasoning. The economics of it dictate that I continue working to continue working. My illusions of grandeur shrivel to a pile of well-formed, yet slow-to-implement remnants of what I should be doing. And at some point of my reckoning I succumb to perspective – keeping oddly positive about those situations clearly out of my control. Like the dried remnants…with a shift of perspective they garner new light as dehydrated intentions. So, in essence, they are simply in storage until the timing correlates with the water supply in order to bring those intentions back to life.

Meanwhile, I am eluding the happenstances that squeeze the energy and vitality from my limbs. It is not that I have no plans – only that I have far too many for a day. A new moon occurred just the other day as I was busy stoking the stove. It is as if each time I turn around, someone has grown or moved, or is in the process of transitioning to something, someone or to somewhere else.

I am standing still.

It passes too quickly and not fast enough.

Angels in the Wings

I summon the courage to leash myself to a phone line, clipping the curtailed wire to my scarf and get on my best "I am a state agent" voice as I answer calls. This being day two of living life like Freyda Perrl it isn't very bad. I've noticed I'm smiling more, judging less and kicking my feet whenever I get excited. So far I have made excellent efforts at living life like I was nearly six months old.

Ring Ring* … "call from Claims" comes the automated voice. I run through my introduction to find the gentleman on the other end is a retired State Trooper – a man whom I know personally. He has answered many a call from me with my residence being in his jurisdiction and luck of him being on the other end of my cries for assistance. Keep in mind this was during a time when domestic situations were a daily occurrence; some violent, most heart-breaking, and many of them involving a very young, innocent boy.

In any event, I verify his call and then cross into a "Hey, I know you!" conversation. I explain who I am and my recollection of him as he banters back and forth reminiscing on who I might be as he can't see my face. He remembered and gasps with a, "I have been looking for you!" Thirty-four years on the job with every level of perpetrator in his crosshairs of justice, and he has been looking for me?

"I've looked for you," he exclaims. "You were here and then, all of a sudden, you were gone. I would go to where you used to work and describe you because I couldn't remember your name. No one would give me any information as to your whereabouts, so I figured they were protecting you because of how violent your ex was. But here you are."

We followed up our conversation with me wishing him luck with his new endeavors and him congratulating me for getting out alive.

I paused.

There really are angels out there, masquerading as regular people yet serving to protect others. He must have impacted the ebb and flow of my life – like the butterfly effect – at points outside my call to my fellow NYS agency. There is no way that he could not have. Investment of energy, even of thinking; is impacting another person's life. And only now, almost a decade later do I find out that he was quite significant to me being where I am today. He has had some impact on my health, most-definitely my mental well-being and maybe even my survival.

My birthday being a few days ago, and at the commencement of reaching thirty-three the thought occurred to me that Jesus was sacrificed at thirty-three. An awakening that maybe I had not accomplished all that I set out to do at 18 – not nearly as much as Jesus had done by this age. Hysteria of having my life to this point marked with a large, red "F" took hold and I froze. My thoughts stayed only in that thread…what have you done? What do you aspire to do?

…to help, to feed and nourish, to aide and support, to encourage, assist and fight for those I love; for the under-represented, the discouraged and the sad. To change fear to strength and work from the inside-out while making the outside shine. That is what I want to do. But how? What does that all mean? On a higher level of understanding, I feel that I have done that; am doing that - particularly after processing my phone call. I have expended energy, love and care toward those that encircle my life. Still, it is not enough. I am ravaged by this urge to do what I am, not just be what I do.

Drawn. I am drawn to a calling not yet found.

Drive.

There are a handful of ways to progress: determination, zest, passion, and in my humble opinion, drive. Drive, in this manner, is not to be confused with determination, as it is fueled by another element outside of determination. I have subscribed to determination for the better part of a decade. It is the formula of twice the "no's" to the "that's impossible", mixed in equal parts to a self-made "there has to be more than this" mixture. That has worked many times that I have felt it would not. Drive, however, is a whole other beast. Drive is feeling and ambition mixed with solid, 140-proof kick-your-ass awesomeness.

I stumbled upon drive recently. Unexpectedly actually. Come to find out, I am without zest if not for failure. And as life would have it, I have failed. A lot. Drive appeared at the intersection of this is how amazing your life is (just out of reach) and that blase feeling of going through the motions day after day. My internal workings operate most of the time on formulas. I wouldn't call them math formulas, or even of a chemical nature. They're life mixtures of circumstances to experience. My drive comes in small, stabbing, insecurity measures of an "I may be less than thou" facade, and I fain at the time I will not feel that = drive. Drive, as one would have it in the day and life of an antiquated letter-writer, socially-soluble listener of issues, and want-er for the best and better of all for everyone, woman of my stature - is a well practiced skit in the Ego. I don't like ego, so this is a *huge* deal. My entrance on stage during the first airing of "Drive" involves my right eye being squinted, left hip out with hand upon it (nails are probably painted cherry red) and the heels I don are the neon orange ones that speak to my second and third layers of personality. In this presentation, my other identity is unafraid, absolutely not insecure, ...unhinged. My hair is big - in a Farrah Fawcet kind of way, and my smile does not elude to the thoughts that would be fondling themselves while sifting through old ashes.

Damn ashes.

Burned and still rendering ...

No, not rendering. They're dead. This is drive, after all. Drive in its present form is one helluva mastermind. That siren red lipstick is going to be a daily occurrence, and the plan meeting drive is unabashed, completely assured, and salable. Going to work on delineating what needs to be the constant: food, for one. Food brings friends. Friends bring stories. And stories bring support (this is assuming the food is good). My food is good. Drivers have good food. Hang on, woman with drive...does that mean I'm a driver? I'm a good driver for that matter. Either way - my fingernails may have dirt beneath the nail bed, and my feet will most definitely contain earth-matter, but I will still be polished. To the point that seeking "drive" is going to be on everyone's next best doers list. Sign on up; I love company and I could use a hand in maintaining focus.

Chickens: Crossing the Road

I want to say that I didn't start out all insecure and scared; synonymous with the turtle who has yet to cross the road. I began in much the same way we all do.

I was born.

That in and of itself, was enough. I was born, breathing, screaming, a crying mess unto myself - but born. Alive.

And now? Now, at some point in my existence of experience, I have been tainted. I have become accustomed to disappointment, to outrage, to upset and lies. I have tendencies toward mistrust and criticism. I blame myself and work consistently toward understanding those things that lie deep beneath the surface of my skin.

In some manner I always seem to return to this place. It adds a touch of comfort; of familiarity. And yet - I recall listing my faults, burning them accordingly and resolving to stop accepting such self-prescribed criticism. It is as Einstein referenced when he said, "A hundred times every day I remind myself that my inner and outer life are based on the labors of other men, living and dead, and that I must exert myself in order to give in the same measure as I have received and am still receiving...(Einstein, p. 8-11)".

I do receive. Just what is necessary to become the next evolution of my former being. The catch between are the efforts necessary to become that next evolved persona. I am stymied.

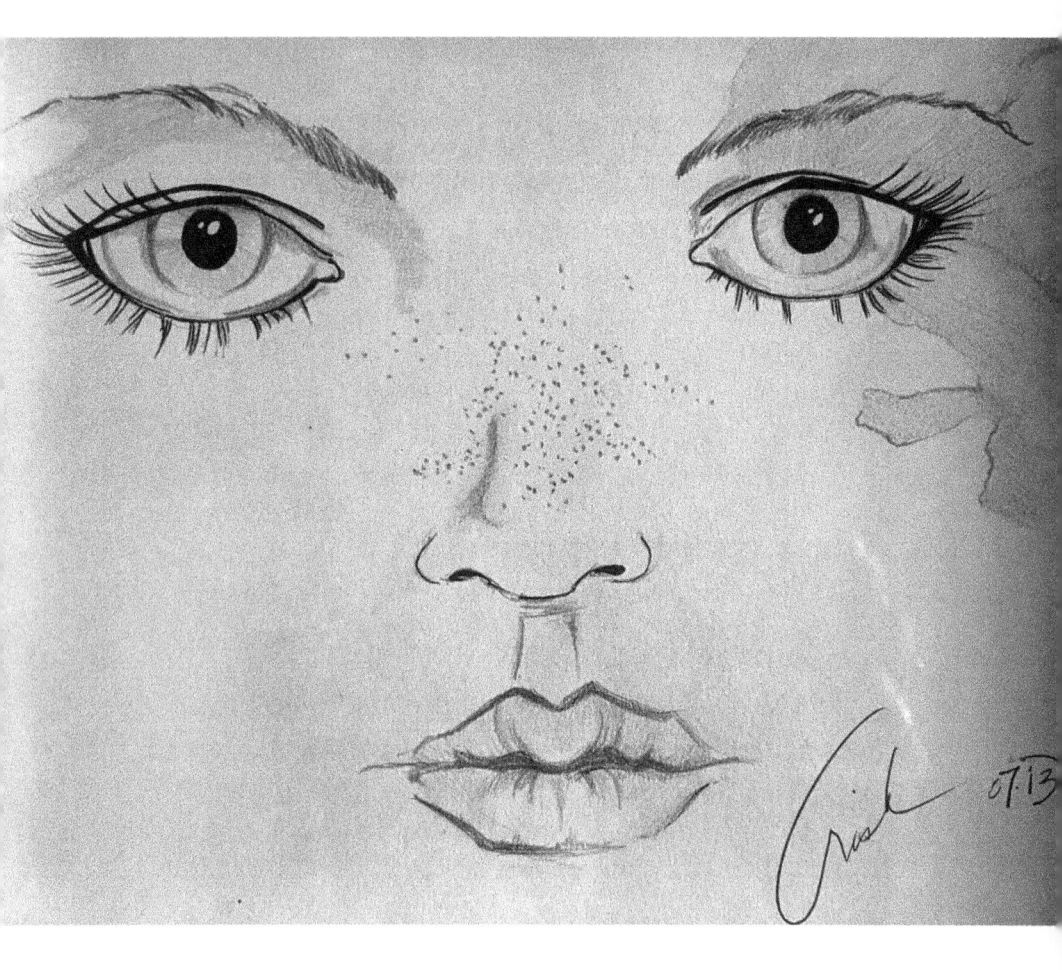

My reflections speak to a time four years ago. My efforts protrude into the next decade, and, I might add, they are quite productive. The here and now is where I falter. The attempt to know more about others than I do myself. I became accustomed to defining the "norm" and counted on my misgivings of the self. I have such a fond recollection of the power of self. My self. I truly feel that Webster did no favor to connect words for the sake of saving on printing costs. In my mind, myself is two words.

Two words.

A pleasure versus pain motif. Nothing exists in one realm without the imparting of the other. The entirety of my point being that there is a formula to all of this. The age-old adage about some chicken and some road. Why? Why did that particular chicken cross that particular road?

Because there is a longing to reach the places no chicken is supposed to go. Big, vast, desirous places that the individual longs to explore for the sake of being a better person. The catch being that we don't know what that exploration of the soul may produce until we do the work for ... self.

Einstein, A. (1954). Ideas and Opinions, based on Mein Weltbild. P. 8-11, http://www.aip.org/history/exhibits/einstein/essay.htm

So Damn Special

She called it the spin-cycle.

The nomenclature attached to the feeling of being simply out of control with those thoughts and emotions that so swiftly carried her to a place she did not care for. In some ways it was a necessary pattern of reconciling with the forces of her depths - while in other ways, and more particularly, bothersome ways, it was an irritant of immeasurable proportions.

"It is the thought process that evokes the spin-cycle," she thought.

If only I could stop thinking...

And then the phone rang.

With too many things to consider, far too many elements to choose from, and not nearly enough time for them all - I stumbled toward the clang on the counter. Why is it that this blessed phone jingles when I have finally reached a point of conscious thought?

Faith spoke to me from the other end of my tyrannical perspective and we covered all the ground that lies between what we think and how we feel, to the inevitability of our thoughts acting on our motions. Funny how faith is. Turns out Faith was contending with much the same things.

In two and a half hours I covered the ground of how she is feeling; mirrored by what I experienced and had all the advice to hand over, just not apply.

(INSERT Rest here)

"You've done it before and you can do it now. See the positive possibilities. Redirect the substantial energy of your frustration and turn it into positive, effective, unstoppable determination."~ Ralph Marston

About Those Pain Receptors

Pain is unrecognizable to those souls living life in fresh perspective.

Babies.

To the rest of us, it is an expected grievance.

Elements of pain come in forms of the physical, the mental, psychological, the physiological...the emotional. The happenstance affects every part.

I was born unafraid. Courageous, even. And now - I sat through October; my anniversary - expectant of life. Thoughtful toward what my amazing husband of a man and I could create. We were pregnant. Able. All that we had planned and thought of had finally come to a point of culmination.

I bled.

For forty-two days.

Two methotrexate (cancer-drug) treatments and four months later, I still wreak the havoc of what it means to be a perfectionist-idealist-mother-to-be...grieving. For months I put off the grieving. I replaced it with what I might do for someone else. Quite an accomplished time, if i might say.

116 days.

That is the studied length of time that Methotrexate stays in the tissue of the body. I (often) hate myself. I want for things I cannot control. I dream of things I cannot give right now. I long for serenity.

That peace that I have worked so hard for...diligently for. I want my peace back.

I create. Out of what appears as hopeless, lost, unadventured or misinterpreted. I compose. And yet, I am left; longing...debilitated and sad. In time, in long lengths of time, I am able to recompose. But really - I am sad.

An aching, longing, nag pulls at me. I want to do more, be more, become more. I cannot.

If I sit. A big if...I sleep.

If I think for just a moment with my tea, I sleep. In eleven hours - I accomplished a plethora of dreams, a recollection of plans and one sky-diving mission of which I was unaware in my slumber. But dammit, if I didn't become it.

And in the day - I fail. I cannot possibly be all that I need to be when those persons entrusted to my care come to depend on me. I am technically savvy, emotionally available, and with motherly instincts to beat the band (most days) but lately - LEAVE ME ALONE is all I can muster as a response.

Culmination.

Of emotion.

Sucks.

My "Be better; do better...with what you have, at the time" slogan is sadly lacking as of late.

Tomorrow - I will be better. Until then -

slumber....

Retreat

Her fingers danced among the thorns, plucking ripeness from its perch.

The fruits of her labors
      so abundantly delicious.

Though she was a novice at life
      She considered herself refined in the art of living.

There were other ways; certainly
Yet hers was a place of fortified faith

The belief that should she be consistently committed, all rewards would be bestowed.
Thorns, like weeds - had their place.
      Their distinctiveness in growth was beset only by the brush strokes of color framing poignant efforts to be alive.

And from this, she gained the dignity of living well. Living with complete exhaustion of all endeavors toward excellence. Surely, any effort would yield some crop.
That largesse, her proof of enhancing to an excellent being.

Groups of Girls

Women. We are a quizzical beast. We hide, we box and we bury those thoughts that bother. I can speak only to the nature that I experience and yet, I am defeated by my thoughts.

= why?

Those situations that claim life, the ones that become larger than

us; they just happen. We don't always get to find out why and this becomes the bother.

I exist in a space where I can fight. Yet, I should not always be on such posed awareness. I feel as though there are times and places to ready the sword; the verbal lashing. And this does not need to be an always thing.

I reexamine this thread over a span of four years post initiation.

Not really sure what to believe; I write.

I have been asked to respond to a matter of three questions each defining happiness or need in my individual manner of speaking. According to yesterday's front my emails suggested that I was in the throes of "willful ignorance," the idea that I deliberately avoid evidence that is contrary to my own belief systems. I would say that this is true to a degree. I avoid pain. I find a word-around for the things that might bring me upset, anxiety or frustration, if I can. Don't we all? At this very same time, I know how to rise when I need to. I understand that preparation for the worst case scenario is better than an unprepared life, and also that I should count my blessings more often than I tally my woes.

The catch here is that tallying your woes is easy.

Negative things that occur exist in the forefront of our focus.

If someone were to ask us "what's wrong?" we could rattle off a ready-made mental listing of all the things that are not right.

"I can't sleep because I lay awake worrying. My mind is full of things that could go wrong, maybe someone lost a job, has to work from home, isn't going to get paid, there are no classes, I can't access the things I need to access, I'm concerned about food, my friends, my family. I don't understand why this is all happening, and I have no one to talk to about it..." The list goes on. Concerted efforts could probably keep it going indefinitely.

But what does that do? What relief does all that "stuffing" of thoughts and emotions do for you? For us?

Nothing.

It brings no relief, no peace of mind. Worrying does not assist breathing or sleep patterns. There is no wellness to be had from the weight of worry.

I return to the question(s) at hand: What does happiness mean to you? What do you need more of in your life?

Happiness = peace of mind. Peace of mind = not worrying, and not worrying = taking one breath at a time while focusing and refocusing my brain.

It's like the quote:

For the time being, I am testing my own brain against my breath. And what might I need more of?

Breaths.

www.ingramcontent.com/pod-product-compliance
Lightning Source LLC
Chambersburg PA
CBHW050929240426
43671CB00020B/2971